2003 | General

[BLANK PAGE]

G

1540/402

NATIONAL
QUALIFICATIONS
2003

MONDAY, 12 MAY
10.20 AM – 11.50 AM

HISTORY
STANDARD GRADE
General Level

Answer questions from Unit I **and** Unit II **and** Unit III.

Choose only **one** Context from each Unit and answer Sections A **and** B. The Contexts chosen should be those you have studied.

The Contexts in each Unit are:

You must use the information in the sources, and your own knowledge, to answer the questions.

Number the questions as shown in the question paper.

Some sources have been adapted or translated.

SCOTTISH
QUALIFICATIONS
AUTHORITY

Marks

UNIT I—CHANGING LIFE IN SCOTLAND AND BRITAIN

CONTEXT A: 1750s–1850s

SECTION A: KNOWLEDGE AND UNDERSTANDING

Study the information in the sources. You must also use your own knowledge in your answers.

Source A describes work in a cotton mill.

Source A

> Factory employment was very different. Costly machinery had to be used on a continuous basis and that meant long hours and a strict supervision of labour. In the cotton mills, even night work was not unknown when trade was brisk. Workers normally laboured for six days a week.

1. Describe working conditions in a cotton mill.   4

Source B is about farm housing from the memoirs of Dr James Russell.

Source B

> The cottages for the shepherds in the Scottish Borders were little better than dark, smoky hovels. Their walls were made of stone and turf and their floor of earth. A hole in the middle of the roof was the only chimney and rain or snow sometimes entered this open space.

2. How serious a problem was poor housing for farming families in Lowland and Border Scotland?   3

Marks

SECTION B: ENQUIRY SKILLS

The issue for investigating is:

> The Clearances brought benefits for the evicted Highlanders.

Study the sources carefully and answer the questions which follow.

You should use your own knowledge where appropriate.

Source C is by Patrick Sellar who was factor of the Sutherland estates in the early nineteenth century.

Source C

> Look inside one of the newly built fishermen's cottages, where the evicted Highlanders have been settled, and you will see the man and his wife and his young children weaving their nets around the winter fire. Contrast that with the poverty and filth of an unevicted tenant's turf hut. You cannot say that these men have been injured by civilisation. They are well off.

3. How useful is **Source C** for investigating the effects of the Highland Clearances? **3**

Source D was written by the Rev. Donald Sage who witnessed a clearance.

Source D

> It was the month of April, 1819, that they were all on one day to quit their cottages and go. For some, a few miserable patches of ground were given out as plots, without anything in the shape of the poorest hut to shelter them. Upon these plots it was decided that they should farm the ground and occupy themselves as fishermen, although the great majority had never set foot in a boat in their lives.

4. What evidence in **Source C** agrees with the view that the Clearances brought benefits for the evicted Highlanders?

What evidence in **Source D** suggests that life for evicted Highlanders was not good? **5**

5. How far do you agree that the Clearances brought benefits for the evicted Highlanders?

You must use evidence **from the sources** and **your own knowledge** to come to a conclusion. **4**

[END OF CONTEXT IA]

Now turn to the Context you have chosen in Unit II.

Marks

UNIT I—CHANGING LIFE IN SCOTLAND AND BRITAIN

CONTEXT B: 1830s–1930s

SECTION A: KNOWLEDGE AND UNDERSTANDING

Study the information in the sources. You must also use your own knowledge in your answers.

Source A is an eyewitness account of farming improvements in East Lothian in the nineteenth century.

Source A

> There was hardly any waste ground. It was all planted with crops. All the fields were straight and tidy looking. I had never seen anything like it. Red roofed steadings with smoke coming from their chimneys was evidence that threshing was taking place. Every farm had its steam engine and threshing machinery.

1. Describe the changes which had taken place in farming in the nineteenth century.　　　**4**

Source B is about housing in a rural area in the late nineteenth century.

Source B

> In the countryside, rows of reasonably solid stone or brick cottages appeared on almost every farm. They would each have a stone or a wooden floor and a fireplace. Before long, they would also all have running water.

2. How important were the improvements made to rural housing by the late nineteenth century?　　　**3**

Marks

SECTION B: ENQUIRY SKILLS

The issue for investigating is:

> The Scots who emigrated in the nineteenth century had a better standard of living than at home.

Study the sources carefully and answer the questions which follow.

You should use your own knowledge where appropriate.

Source C was written by Simon Fraser who emigrated to Australia from Inverness. It was published in the "Inverness Courier" in 1854.

Source C

> Tell all to come here where they get good wages and not to be starving at home as they do. I was at Melbourne and was offered £10 per week but I hope to get £12 per week. This is the country to live in. In six months I will be an independent man. Everyone that works hard will do well here.

3. How useful is **Source C** for investigating emigration from Scotland during the nineteenth century?

3

Source D is taken from a letter sent by a Scotsman who emigrated to Australia in the nineteenth century.

Source D

> My daughter has got a job working for a minister for only £10 a year. I could have got her a job with me but I would not allow it, the flour mill being a dangerous place to work. My wages are ten shillings (50p) a week. I work from 6 am until 8 pm. The people here are wishing for rain as it has not rained for seven months. This country is not as good as made out at home.

4. What evidence in **Source C** supports the view that Scots who emigrated had a better standard of living?

   What evidence in **Source D** opposes the view that Scots who emigrated had a better standard of living?

5

5. How far do you agree that the Scots who emigrated in the nineteenth century had a better standard of living than at home?

   You must use evidence **from the sources** and **your own knowledge** to come to a conclusion.

4

[END OF CONTEXT IB]

Now turn to the Context you have chosen in Unit II.

Marks

UNIT I—CHANGING LIFE IN SCOTLAND AND BRITAIN

CONTEXT C: 1880s–Present Day

SECTION A: KNOWLEDGE AND UNDERSTANDING

Study the information in the sources. You must also use your own knowledge in your answers.

Source A describes the development of trade unions in the early twentieth century.

Source A

> Improving working conditions were partly due to the better organised and more numerous trade unions of the time. In the early twentieth century many small unions combined to form bigger unions. What had once been only Scottish unions sometimes merged with English ones.

1. Describe the changes in trade unions in the early twentieth century. **4**

Source B is about rural housing in Caithness in the early twentieth century.

Source B

> They had no piped water supply. Rain or well water was used. There was no indoor sanitation or even an outdoor toilet. Some favourite corner on the hill or in a quarry was used by both men and women. Nor was there a proper bath. A big wooden tub used for the annual washing of blankets could be used for this purpose.

2. How serious a problem was poor rural housing in the early twentieth century? **3**

Marks

SECTION B: ENQUIRY SKILLS

The issue for investigating is:

> Poverty was the main reason why Scots emigrated after 1880.

Study the sources carefully and answer the questions which follow.

You should use your own knowledge where appropriate.

Source C is from a magazine, the "Northern Commercial Journal", published in 1927.

Source C

> One only has to look at the long queues at the Labour Exchange and to read of the many poor, able bodied men who have been given help from the Parish Poor Fund, to know that Fraserburgh has not been flourishing this year. Another sign of the bad times is the steady stream of young men and women to lands beyond the seas in search of a livelihood.

3. How useful is **Source C** for investigating why Scots emigrated in the twentieth century?　　　　　　　**3**

Source D is from "Change in Scotland 1830–1930".

Source D

> People left the country, not because they were pushed, but because they were pulled. Scotland had never been a rich country. Other lands offered the promise of cheap farmland, work for all and the prospect of wealth. Right up to the present day, many skilled Scots have gone abroad in search of jobs.

4. What evidence is there in **Source C** that poverty was a reason for Scots emigrating?

   What evidence is there in **Source D** that there were other reasons for Scots emigrating?　　　　　**5**

5. How far do you agree that poverty was the main reason why Scots emigrated after 1880?

   You must use evidence **from the sources** and **your own knowledge** to come to a conclusion.　　　　　**4**

[END OF CONTEXT IC]

Now turn to the Context you have chosen in Unit II.

Marks

UNIT II—INTERNATIONAL COOPERATION AND CONFLICT

> ### CONTEXT A: 1790s–1820s

SECTION A: KNOWLEDGE AND UNDERSTANDING

Study the information in the sources. You must also use your own knowledge in your answers.

Source A gives evidence about the outbreak of war between Britain and France.

Source A

> In November 1792 the French issued the Edict of Fraternity, calling on all people to overthrow their rulers, just as they had done. The British government's attitude grew much colder towards France: soon they would be at war.

1. Explain why the Edict of Fraternity helped to bring about the war between Britain and France.

3

Source B was written by Robert Hay about his experiences in 1811.

Source B

> The Press Gang took me on board a man-o-war and questioned me. "Are you willing to join the King's Service?" I replied, "No, I can get much better conditions and higher wages in the merchant service and, should I be unable to agree with the Captain, I am free to leave the ship at the end of the voyage."

2. Describe life in the British navy during the wars with France.

3

Marks

SECTION B: ENQUIRY SKILLS

The following sources are about the Congress of Vienna.

Study the sources carefully and answer the questions which follow.

You should use your own knowledge where appropriate.

Source C is from "A New European Balance" by Stephanie Verbeure.

Source C

> Metternich was wrong when he said the Congress of Vienna had redrawn the map of Europe "for all time". The Congress reflected the wishes of the great powers and ignored the national hopes of many people, Italians and Belgians amongst others. This led to trouble in the future. However, the Congress can be praised for not treating defeated France too harshly.

3. What does the author of **Source C** think about the Congress of Vienna?   4

Source D comes from "Modern British History" by Norman Lowe.

Source D

> The major success of the Congress was that there was no major conflict in Europe until 1854. On the other hand, there were criticisms of the settlement. It ignored the principle of nationalism: the people of Belgium were placed under Dutch rule and Italians under Austrian rule. They were placed under foreign governments to suit the wishes of the great powers.

4. How far do **Sources C** and **D** agree about the Congress of Vienna?   4

[END OF CONTEXT IIA]

Now turn to the Context you have chosen in Unit III.

Marks

UNIT II—INTERNATIONAL COOPERATION AND CONFLICT

CONTEXT B: 1890s–1920s

SECTION A: KNOWLEDGE AND UNDERSTANDING

Study the information in the sources. You must also use your own knowledge in your answers.

Source A gives evidence about the Balkans before World War One.

Source A

> Different nationalities were mixed together in the Balkans. Two great powers, Russia and Austria-Hungary, bordered the countries in this region. Both wanted to control the area because it gave them access to the Mediterranean sea.

1. Explain why the situation in the Balkans was a cause of tension in Europe before 1914.   **3**

Source B is about conditions on the Western Front.

Source B

> The trenches stretched from the Swiss Alps to the English Channel. In these trenches, soldiers were often knee-deep in mud. Many were drowned when they slipped into flooded shell holes. When the temperature dropped they suffered from frost-bite.

2. Describe conditions for soldiers in the trenches on the Western Front.   **3**

Marks

SECTION B: ENQUIRY SKILLS

The following sources are about Allied attitudes towards Germany at the end of the war.

Study the sources carefully and answer the questions which follow.

You should use your own knowledge where appropriate.

Source C describes French Prime Minister Clemenceau's views about the Germans in 1918.

Source C

> A German only understands threats. In addition, Germans are without mercy. Therefore you must never negotiate with a German or compromise with him; you must dictate to him otherwise he will not respect you.

3. What does Clemenceau think about the Germans? 4

In **Source D** a British army officer describes his attitude towards the Germans in 1918.

Source D

> The Germans are the most civilised and the most aggressive of European nations. To keep them down for ever would be a hopeless and dangerous task. They will react violently to anything they think is unjust. The Germans should not be treated as underdogs.

4. How far do **Sources C** and **D** agree about the Germans in 1918? 4

[END OF CONTEXT IIB]

Now turn to the Context you have chosen in Unit III.

Marks

UNIT II—INTERNATIONAL COOPERATION AND CONFLICT

CONTEXT C: 1930s–1960s

SECTION A: KNOWLEDGE AND UNDERSTANDING

Study the information in the sources. You must also use your own knowledge in your answers.

Source A is about the events following the Czech Crisis in 1938.

Source A

> Chamberlain's hopes of peace did not survive the winter. As soon as the Czech situation was settled, the German government started pressurising the Poles to force them to agree to the return of Danzig to Germany. At the beginning of 1939 Hitler stepped up the campaign to bring about the complete breakup of Czechoslovakia.

1. Explain in what ways the events after the Czech Crisis increased the tension in Europe.

   3

Source B is from the diary of someone living in Hiroshima when the atomic bomb was dropped.

Source B

> Hundreds of people who were trying to escape to the hills passed our house. The sight of them was almost unbearable. Their faces and hands were burnt and swollen. Sheets of skin had peeled away from their bodies and hung down like rags on a scarecrow.

2. Describe the effects which the atomic bomb had on Japanese civilians.

   3

Marks

SECTION B: ENQUIRY SKILLS

The following sources are about the impact of the United Nations.

Study the sources carefully and answer the questions which follow.

You should use your own knowledge where appropriate.

Source C is from "The United Nations" written by Patrick Rooke in 1966.

Source C

> There have been times when the future of the United Nations looked doubtful. However, the United Nations has proved its value and strength. There have been a number of minor, localised wars, some of which threatened to become major wars, but general peace has been maintained in the world. Today, the United Nations is more firmly established than at any time in its history.

3. What did Patrick Rooke think of the United Nations in 1966?   **4**

In **Source D** Robert Doig describes the progress made by the United Nations up to the 1960s.

Source D

> The initial hopes and plans for the United Nations have been largely achieved since its formation in 1945. No large scale war has threatened the peace of the world and much valuable development work has been completed in many countries by United Nations organisations. There have been tensions between nations and the United Nations has had to deal with them.

4. How far do **Sources C** and **D** agree about the United Nations?   **4**

[END OF CONTEXT IIC]

Now turn to the Context you have chosen in Unit III.

Marks

UNIT III—PEOPLE AND POWER

> ### CONTEXT A: USA 1850–1880

SECTION A: KNOWLEDGE AND UNDERSTANDING

Study the information in the sources. You must also use your own knowledge in your answers.

Source A was written by someone who was worried about the effects of westward expansion.

Source A

> With the stream of emigration westwards, the buffalo will dwindle away. The wandering tribes who depend on them for support will be broken and scattered. The Indians (native Americans) will soon be ruined by whisky and controlled by military posts.

1. Explain some of the ways native Americans (Indians) were affected by westward expansion.

    3

Source B is from Abraham Lincoln's Inaugural Address of 1861.

Source B

> I hold the view that the Union of the States is perpetual. It is impossible to destroy it except by some action not provided for in the Constitution itself. If the Union is a contract between States then that contract cannot be broken by less than all the parties who made it. Any act of violence by one State against the authority of the United States is considered a revolutionary act.

2. How important was the Union to Abraham Lincoln?

    4

SECTION B: ENQUIRY SKILLS

Marks

The following sources are about slavery and the causes of the Civil War.

Study the sources carefully and answer the questions which follow.

You should use your own knowledge where appropriate.

Source C is an advertisement for a runaway slave which was published in a newspaper before the Civil War.

Source C

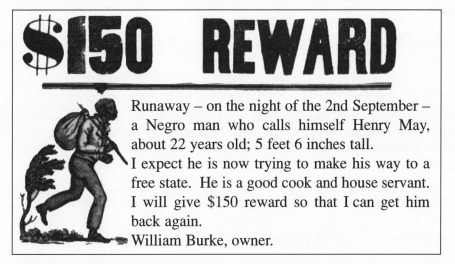

> $150 REWARD
>
> Runaway – on the night of the 2nd September – a Negro man who calls himself Henry May, about 22 years old; 5 feet 6 inches tall.
> I expect he is now trying to make his way to a free state. He is a good cook and house servant. I will give $150 reward so that I can get him back again.
> William Burke, owner.

3. How useful is **Source C** as evidence of the evils of slavery?

4

Source D describes the views contained in anti-slavery petitions.

Source D

> The message of the Abolitionists was always the same. Slavery was a sin and those involved in slavery were sinners who must seek forgiveness immediately. Anyone who refused to speak out against slavery was seen by Abolitionists to be very cowardly.

4. According to the author of **Source D**, what did Abolitionists think about those who did not oppose slavery?

3

Source E is from www.encartaencyclopedia.com

Source E

> The chief cause of the American Civil War was slavery. Southern States depended on slavery to support their economy and were alarmed at any attacks on it. Opponents of slavery were concerned about the expansion of slavery because they did not want to compete against slave labour.

5. How fully does **Source E** explain the causes of the Civil War?

You must use evidence **from the source** and **your own knowledge** to come to a conclusion.

3

[END OF CONTEXT IIIA]

Marks

UNIT III—PEOPLE AND POWER

| CONTEXT B: INDIA 1917–1947 |

SECTION A: KNOWLEDGE AND UNDERSTANDING

Study the information in the sources. You must also use your own knowledge in your answers.

Source A is about some features of British rule in India.

Source A

> Many British officials, after twenty or thirty years service, felt at home in India. They were even devoted to India. However, their very presence was a humiliation to Indians. British rule hurt Indian pride and always strengthened the idea that the Indians were a subject people.

1. Why were many Indians unhappy with British rule in India?   3

Source B describes the role of Nehru.

Source B

> Nehru dedicated his life to the nationalist struggle. He spent nine years in nine different jails. He broadened the appeal of Congress and maintained unity in the party. In one vital respect he had to admit failure. The dream that India would become free and remain united was shattered when independence came.

2. How important was Nehru in the struggle for Indian independence?   4

SECTION B: ENQUIRY SKILLS   *Marks*

The sources below are about Gandhi and unrest in India during British rule.

Study the sources carefully and answer the questions which follow.

You should use your own knowledge where appropriate.

Source C is a newspaper photograph taken in 1930 of Mahatma Gandhi and his supporters on the Salt March.

Source C

3.   How useful is **Source C** as evidence of Gandhi's protests against British rule?   **4**

In **Source D** Gandhi talks about his discontent with the cotton industry in England.

Source D

> Machinery in the past has made us dependent on England. The only way we can rid ourselves of that dependence is to boycott all cloth made by English machinery. That is why we have made it the patriotic duty of every Indian to spin his own cotton. This is our form of attacking a powerful nation like England.

4.   What was Gandhi's attitude towards the production of cotton?   **3**

Source E is from a biography of Mahatma Gandhi.

Source E

> In the 1920s Gandhi went all over India spreading the message that non-cooperation would lead to independence. At huge public meetings he urged the people to give up wearing foreign clothing and to boycott British cloth. In 1929 he started a new campaign of civil disobedience.

5.   How fully does **Source E** describe the tactics used by Gandhi in the campaign for Indian independence?

     Use evidence **from the source** and **your own knowledge** in your answer.   **3**

[END OF CONTEXT IIIB]

UNIT III—PEOPLE AND POWER   *Marks*

| CONTEXT C: RUSSIA 1914–1941 |

SECTION A: KNOWLEDGE AND UNDERSTANDING

Study the information in the sources. You must also use your own knowledge in your answers.

Source A is from "Russia and the USSR, 1905–1956".

Source A

> Tsar Nicholas II ruled over a huge empire. He decided everything relating to Russia's government and the armed forces. The people of Russia had no say in the running of the country. Nicholas received advice from a Committee of Ministers—all of whom were chosen from the nobility by the Tsar himself.

1. Explain some of the reasons why many Russians disliked the Tsar before 1914.   **3**

Source B is from "Modern World History".

Source B

> The Whites lacked one single leader. Their generals were jealous of each other and refused to attack at the same time. Some White leaders were cruel and this encouraged many Russians to support the Reds.

2. How important was the problem of poor leadership in explaining why the Whites were defeated by the Reds?   **4**

SECTION B: ENQUIRY SKILLS

The following sources are about the problems and downfall of the Provisional Government.

Study the sources carefully and answer the questions which follow.

You should use your own knowledge where appropriate.

Source C was said by a Russian soldier in the autumn of 1917.

Source C

> Show me what we are fighting this war for. Is it for democracy or for the capitalist plunderers? If you can prove to me that I am defending the Revolution then I'll go out and fight—without the threat of a death sentence to force me! When the land belongs to the peasants, and the factories to the workers, and the power to the Soviets, then I'll know we have something to fight for. Then we will fight for it!

3. What does the soldier in **Source C** think about continuing to fight in the war?   **3**

Source D is a photograph of women queuing for food in Petrograd in September 1917.   *Marks*

Source D

4. How useful is **Source D** as evidence of hardship during the time of the Provisional Government?   **4**

Source E is from a modern history textbook.

Source E

> Lenin had spent many years preparing the Bolsheviks for Revolution. He soon became aware that soldiers and civilians disliked the World War. By 1917 he had a small group of dedicated revolutionaries ready and able to seize power. Support for the Bolsheviks increased due to Lenin's slogans.

5. How fully does **Source E** describe the part played by Lenin in the Bolshevik Revolution?

Use evidence **from the source** and **your own knowledge** in your answer.   **3**

[END OF CONTEXT IIIC]

Marks

UNIT III—PEOPLE AND POWER

CONTEXT D: GERMANY 1918–1939

SECTION A: KNOWLEDGE AND UNDERSTANDING

Study the information in the sources. You must also use your own knowledge in your answers.

Source A is about the response in Germany to the Versailles Peace Settlement.

Source A

> There was angry reaction in Germany to the Treaty of Versailles. This was not just because they had been forced to accept the treaty and the punishments it contained. They were angry because many Germans would now have to live under foreign rule and because German-speaking Austria was not allowed to join with Germany.

1. Why were many Germans unhappy with the Versailles Peace Settlement?   3

Source B describes the use of propaganda by the Nazis in the 1930s.

Source B

> The Nazis tried to control all forms of expression and communication. This was done through propaganda and censorship. In overall charge of propaganda was Goebbels who headed the Nazi Ministry of People's Enlightenment and Propaganda, set up in 1933. He controlled the media to spread the Nazi message. Those who ignored the message were made to suffer.

2. How important was Goebbels' propaganda work in controlling the German people?   4

SECTION B: ENQUIRY SKILLS   *Marks*

The following sources are about discontent during the time of the Weimar Republic.

Study the sources carefully and answer the questions which follow.

You should use your own knowledge where appropriate.

Source C shows workers collecting their wages in washing baskets during the hyperinflation crisis of 1923.

Source C

3. How useful is **Source C** as evidence of the problems of hyperinflation?   **4**

Source D was written by a German in 1932.

Source D

> By supporting National Socialism we were showing our hatred of parliamentary politics and democratic debate. We showed we were against all the higgling and haggling of the other parties, their coalitions and their confusions. It was a common man's rejection of "the rascals". The cry was "Throw them all out."

4. What was the attitude of the author of **Source D** towards political parties in Germany?   **3**

Source E describes the situation in Germany in the early 1930s.

Source E

> The effects of the 1929 Wall Street Crash were keenly felt into the 1930s. As unemployment grew and the dole queues lengthened, so many Germans grew more and more angry with the Weimar politicians. Increasingly, the promises of Hitler proved attractive to many Germans and they turned in their thousands to the Nazis.

5. How fully does **Source E** show why German people turned against the Weimar politicians in the 1930s?

    Use evidence **from the source** and **your own knowledge** in your answer.   **3**

[END OF CONTEXT IIID]

[END OF QUESTION PAPER]

[BLANK PAGE]

[BLANK PAGE]

C

1540/403

NATIONAL
QUALIFICATIONS
2003

MONDAY, 12 MAY
1.00 PM – 2.45 PM

HISTORY
STANDARD GRADE
Credit Level

Answer questions from Unit I **and** Unit II **and** Unit III.

Choose only **one** Context from each Unit and answer Sections A **and** B. The Contexts chosen should be those you have studied.

The Contexts in each Unit are:

Number the questions as shown in the question paper.

Some sources have been adapted or translated.

SCOTTISH
QUALIFICATIONS
AUTHORITY

©

Marks

UNIT I—CHANGING LIFE IN SCOTLAND AND BRITAIN

> ### CONTEXT A: 1750s–1850s

SECTION A: KNOWLEDGE AND UNDERSTANDING

> After 1750 many Scottish landowners began to improve the old run rig system of farming.

1. Explain why farming methods improved after 1750.   **5**

> Before 1832 the number of people who could vote in Scotland was very restricted.

2. Describe the improvements to democracy in Scotland made by the 1832 Reform Act.   **4**

SECTION B: ENQUIRY SKILLS

The issue for investigating is:

> Better medical knowledge was the main cause of population growth in Scotland between 1750 and 1850.

Study the sources carefully and answer the questions which follow.
You should use your own knowledge where appropriate.

Source A is from "Changing Life in Scotland and Britain" by historians R. Cameron, C. Henderson and C. Robertson, published in 1997.

Source A

> Medical knowledge made significant progress during the 19th century. Vaccinating people against smallpox had been discovered by Edward Jenner in 1796. Deaths from smallpox fell from about 3000 per million in 1800 to 500 per million in 1840. James Simpson perfected the use of chloroform as the first reasonably safe and effective anaesthetic for childbirth and surgery. These developments were a factor in the falling death rate.

Source B is taken from the New Statistical Account for Dundee, 1833.

Source B

> The cause of this extraordinary increase in population is due to the great growth of the linen trade which has produced so many spinning mills. By giving employment to thousands it has encouraged early marriages (and more children), as well as bringing families from other parts of Scotland and from Ireland.

Marks

Source C is from "The New Penguin History of Scotland" published in 2001.

Source C

> Between 1750 and 1850 the population of Scotland experienced unprecedented growth. From 1750 annual growth in numbers jumped to 1·2 per cent. Excellent by contemporary standards though Scottish medicine was, it contributed little to the fading away of epidemic diseases. Bubonic plague just ceased to happen while better quarantine procedures prevented its reintroduction. Improved incomes by 1800 may have enhanced diet.

3. How useful are **Sources A** and **B** for investigating the causes of population rise in Scotland between 1750 and 1850?

   4

Look at Sources A, B and C.

4. What evidence is there in the sources to support the view that better medical knowledge caused population growth in Scotland?

   What evidence is there in the sources to suggest that there were other reasons for population growth in Scotland?

   6

5. How far do you agree that better medical knowledge was the main cause of population growth in Scotland between 1750 and 1850?

   You must use **evidence from the sources** and **your own knowledge** to reach a balanced conclusion.

   5

[END OF CONTEXT IA]

Marks

UNIT I—CHANGING LIFE IN SCOTLAND AND BRITAIN

CONTEXT B: 1830s–1930s

SECTION A: KNOWLEDGE AND UNDERSTANDING

> The coming of the railways brought new opportunities to many people in Scotland.

1. Explain why many people benefitted from the coming of the railways.   5

> It was from the leisured middle classes that the demand for votes for women first came.

2. Describe the non violent methods used by women to campaign for the vote.   4

SECTION B: ENQUIRY SKILLS

The issue for investigating is:

> Population growth between 1830 and 1930 was largely due to medical factors.

Study the sources carefully and answer the questions which follow.
You should use your own knowledge where appropriate.

Source A is statistical evidence from the Registrar General's returns in 1884.

Source A

> The expectation of life is three years longer now than for the previous period of seventeen years ending in 1884. This increase in the length of life is probably due to the abolition of the duty on soap. It has been helped by the ending of the window tax, as well as by improvement to the water supply.

Marks

Source B is from "A Century of the Scottish People" by Professor T. C. Smout, published in 1986.

Source B

> Much of the improvement in infant mortality since 1900 might be attributed to the gradual decrease, since 1870, in the overwork, malnutrition and serious disease of girls and young women. This was assisted in the twentieth century by the introduction of medical inspection in schools and also to general improvements in medical care during and after birth itself.

Source C is from "The Scottish Nation 1700–2000" by T. M. Devine, published in 1999.

Source C

> The direct causes of mortality decline included the control and then the steady reduction of lethal diseases of childhood. This was achieved by improvement of the urban environment through the provision of cleaner water and better sewerage. The efforts of doctors, nurses and midwives were also beginning to be felt in working class communities.

3. How useful are **Sources A** and **B** for investigating the causes of population growth between 1830 and 1930?

   4

Look at Sources A, B and C.

4. What evidence is there in the sources to support the view that medical factors were a cause of population growth?

   What evidence is there in the sources to suggest that there were other reasons for population growth in Scotland?

   6

5. How far do you agree that population growth between 1830 and 1930 was largely due to medical factors?

   You must use **evidence from the sources** and **your own knowledge** to reach a balanced conclusion.

   5

[END OF CONTEXT IB]

Marks

UNIT I—CHANGING LIFE IN SCOTLAND AND BRITAIN

CONTEXT C: 1880s–Present Day

SECTION A: KNOWLEDGE AND UNDERSTANDING

> The shipyards of the Clyde were in deep trouble by the 1970s.

1. Explain why Scottish shipbuilding was in trouble by the 1970s. **5**

> It was from the leisured middle classes that the demand for votes for women first came.

2. Describe the non violent methods used by women to campaign for the vote. **4**

SECTION B: ENQUIRY SKILLS

The issue for investigating is:

> Better health care was the main cause of population growth between 1880 and 1980.

Study the sources carefully and answer the questions which follow. You should use your own knowledge where appropriate.

Source A is from an official medical report to the Government published in 1972.

Source A

> A century ago tuberculosis was the most fatal of all diseases in Britain. It killed many children. In 1900 the death rate due to tuberculosis was 360 in every 1000 of the population. Today that figure has fallen to 10 for men and 3 for women in every 1000. Many factors have contributed to these results: better diet, earlier diagnosis through mass X-rays and the success of the B.C.G. vaccination campaign.

Marks

Source B is an extract from "A Social and Economic History of Industrial Britain" by John Robottom, published in 1986.

Source B

> Since 1948 the most obvious cause of a rising population has been the final victory against fevers which killed thousands as recently as fifty years ago. Immunisation has wiped out diphtheria and typhoid. For a time, there were growing numbers of victims of polio until it was beaten by new vaccines. Rising living standards and free medical treatment have brought about a big improvement in general health and consequent population growth.

Source C is an extract from "British Economic and Social History" by Philip Sauvain, published in 1988.

Source C

> Improvements in living standards and nursing care helped to bring the death rate down in the early years of the twentieth century. In the last thirty years, the decline of heavy industry, the introduction of effective legislation to minimise air pollution and the use of antibiotics have all helped to reduce the incidence of disease and have brought down the death rate still further.

3. How useful are **Sources A** and **B** for investigating the causes of population growth between 1880 and 1980?　　　　4

Look at Sources A, B and C.

4. What evidence is there in the sources to support the view that better health care was a cause of population growth between 1880 and 1980?

   What evidence is there in the sources that other factors caused population growth between 1880 and 1980?　　　　6

5. How far do you agree that better health care was the main cause of population growth between 1880 and 1980?

   You must use **evidence from the sources** and **your own knowledge** to reach a balanced conclusion.　　　　5

[END OF CONTEXT IC]

Marks

UNIT II—INTERNATIONAL COOPERATION AND CONFLICT

CONTEXT A: 1790s–1820s

SECTION A: KNOWLEDGE AND UNDERSTANDING

In both Britain and France, the long war seriously affected the civilian population.

(Note: for this answer you should write a short essay of several paragraphs.)

1. How far do you agree that during the Napoleonic Wars the difficulty of food supply was the most important problem faced by

EITHER

(*a*) civilians in Britain?   8

OR

(*b*) civilians in France?   8

SECTION B: ENQUIRY SKILLS

The following sources are about George Canning and the Congress System.

Study the sources carefully and answer the questions which follow.
You should use your own knowledge where appropriate.

Source A is part of an official instruction written by George Canning, British Foreign Minister at the Congress of Verona in 1822.

Source A

> If there is a proposal to interfere by force in the present struggle in Spain, so convinced is the British Government of the danger of such interference, that you must say that Britain will not agree to participate with the other Congress powers in such interference.

2. How useful is **Source A** as evidence of Britain's attitude to the Congress System?   4

Marks

Source B is from "Europe Since Napoleon" by David Thompson.

Source B

> At the Congress of Verona in 1822, Britain was represented by George Canning whose hostility to congresses and armed intervention into other states was even stronger than that of Castlereagh whom he had had replaced as Foreign Minister. Canning's firm resistance to intervention stopped the members of the Congress System from taking any action in Spain. Canning's complaints at Verona marked the completion of the breach between Britain and her Congress partners.

3. Discuss David Thompson's opinions of George Canning at the Congress of Verona.   **4**

Source C is from a biography of George Canning.

Source C

> George Canning was recalled to the Foreign Office after Castlereagh's death. He reversed previous policy towards the Holy Alliance and refused to cooperate with other Congress partners if it meant intervening into other countries to put down revolutions. He protested about many of the decisions at the Congress of Verona but was unable to prevent French intervention in Spain.

4. How far do **Sources B** and **C** agree about George Canning at the Congress of Verona?   **4**

[END OF CONTEXT IIA]

Marks

UNIT II—INTERNATIONAL COOPERATION AND CONFLICT

CONTEXT B: 1890s–1920s

SECTION A: KNOWLEDGE AND UNDERSTANDING

In both Britain and Germany, the years of war took their toll on the civilian population.

(Note: for this answer you should write a short essay of several paragraphs.)

1. How far do you agree that during the First World War, the difficulty of food supply was the most important problem faced by

    EITHER

    (*a*) civilians in Britain?   **8**

    OR

    (*b*) civilians in Germany?   **8**

SECTION B: ENQUIRY SKILLS

The following sources are about the League of Nations.

Study the sources carefully and answer the questions which follow.
You should use your own knowledge where appropriate.

Source A is part of a speech made by Arthur Balfour, chief British representative at the League of Nations in 1920.

Source A

The League of Nations is not set up to deal with a world in chaos, or with any part of the world which is in trouble. The League of Nations may give assistance but it is not, and cannot be, a complete instrument for bringing order out of chaos.

2. How useful is **Source A** as evidence of attitudes towards the League of Nations?   **4**

Marks

Source B is from "The League of Nations" by historians Gibbons and Morican.

Source B

> The League, handicapped as it was by the absence of major powers, did achieve a measure of success during the Corfu crisis. The League had been designed to deal with just such a dangerous problem as this. It had acted fairly and promptly and it had condemned the violence of the Italians towards the Greeks. But it had lost the initiative. The result was that a great power had once again got away with using force against a small power.

3. Discuss the attitude of the authors of **Source B** towards the League of Nations.   4

Source C is from "World History from 1914" by Christopher Culpin.

Source C

> The most serious blow was the refusal of the USA to become a member. The League was consequently weakened when it came to dealing with incidents such as the Corfu crisis. The League quickly discussed the matter and offered a solution. However, under pressure from the Italian dictator, Mussolini, the terms of the agreement were altered in favour of Italy. The League had been ready to act but the Great Powers acted on their own, ignoring the League. Bullying tactics had paid off.

4. How far do **Sources B** and **C** agree about the League of Nations?   4

[END OF CONTEXT IIB]

Marks

UNIT II—INTERNATIONAL COOPERATION AND CONFLICT

> ### CONTEXT C: 1930s–1960s

SECTION A: KNOWLEDGE AND UNDERSTANDING

> In both Britain and Germany, the long war took its toll on the civilian population.

(Note: for this answer you should write a short essay of several paragraphs.)

1. How far do you agree that during the Second World War, the difficulty of food supply was the most important problem faced by

EITHER

(a) civilians in Britain?   **8**

OR

(b) civilians in Germany?   **8**

SECTION B: ENQUIRY SKILLS

The following sources are about the Berlin Crisis of 1948.

**Study the sources carefully and answer the questions which follow.
You should use your own knowledge where appropriate.**

Source A was published by the Soviet News Agency, "Tass", in May 1948.

Source A

> All road and rail routes into Berlin are now closed. The Soviet authorities are ready to provide food and fuel for the population of the whole of Berlin, but the Western powers are depriving the inhabitants of help from Eastern Germany. The USA are apparently organising a so-called "airlift" which just serves their purposes of propaganda.

2. How useful is **Source A** as evidence of the tensions during the Berlin Blockade?   **4**

Marks

Source B was said at a public meeting by President Truman of America in 1949.

Source B

> We refused to be forced out of the city of Berlin. We demonstrated to the people of Europe that we would act and act firmly when their freedom was threatened. The airlift was a great success in supplying food and fuel to the people of Berlin. Politically, the airlift brought the people of Western Europe closer to us. The Berlin Blockade was a move by the Russians to test our ability and our will to resist.

3. Discuss the attitude of President Truman to the Berlin crisis.   4

Source C is a Soviet commentary on the Berlin crisis.

Source C

> The crisis was planned in Washington. In 1948 there was real danger of war. The conduct of the Western powers risked bloody incidents. The self blockade of the Western powers hit the West Berlin population with harshness. The people were freezing and starving. In the spring of 1949 the USA was forced to yield—their war plans had come to nothing, because of the conduct of the USSR.

4. How far do **Sources B** and **C** agree about the Berlin crisis?   4

[END OF CONTEXT IIC]

Marks

UNIT III—PEOPLE AND POWER

CONTEXT A: USA 1850–1880

SECTION A: KNOWLEDGE AND UNDERSTANDING

> Most Americans could not accept the Mormons as they were quite different.

1. In what ways were the Mormons different from other Americans?　　　3

> The Republicans fought a clear campaign that appealed to many in the North.

2. Explain the reasons why people in the North voted for the Republican Party in 1860.　　　4

SECTION B: ENQUIRY SKILLS

The following sources relate to the period of Reconstruction.

Study the sources carefully and answer the questions which follow.
You should use your own knowledge where appropriate.

Source A was written in a letter to President Johnson from an imprisoned Southern senator.

Source A

> You are no enemy of the South. By your wise and noble statesmanship you have become the benefactor of the Southern people in the time of their greatest need. You have entitled yourself to the gratitude of those living and those yet to live.

3. Discuss the attitude of the author of **Source A** towards President Johnson.　　　4

Marks

Source B describes life in the South during Reconstruction.

Source B

> New opportunities were quickly seized by the Blacks. They set up farms and businesses and went to school and university. This alarmed the Southern whites and many joined anti-Black organisations. There were murders, rapes and whippings. There was also increased discrimination as Whites gave Blacks the worst jobs. Although Blacks were entitled to vote, armed gangs of Whites sometimes stopped them.

4. How fully does **Source B** describe the problems faced by Blacks during the period of Reconstruction in the South?

   You must use **evidence from the source** and **your own knowledge** and give reasons for your answer.   5

[END OF CONTEXT IIIA]

Marks

UNIT III—PEOPLE AND POWER

CONTEXT B: INDIA 1917–1947

SECTION A: KNOWLEDGE AND UNDERSTANDING

Gandhi described events at Amritsar as "an act of inhumanity and vengeance".

1. Describe the events at Amritsar in April 1919.　　　3

Lord Irwin, Viceroy of India announced that the Simon Commission would investigate the prospects for constitutional change in India.

2. Explain why the setting up of the Simon Commission failed to stop unrest in India.　　　4

SECTION B: ENQUIRY SKILLS

The following sources give evidence about Mountbatten's role in Indian independence.

**Study the sources carefully and answer the questions which follow.
You should use your own knowledge where appropriate.**

Source A was written by Dr Taylor who worked in Bombay when Mountbatten was Viceroy.

Source A

We were very glad that Mountbatten came to India. He put aside all the conventions of being Viceroy and all the uniforms and parades. He was just an ordinary man and willing to meet people at their own level. This was a new idea which really touched the Indians. What pleased Nehru and Gandhi was that Mountbatten was prepared to put all ceremony aside and deal with a problem man to man.

3. Discuss the attitude of Dr Taylor to Mountbatten as Viceroy of India.　　　4

Marks

Source B is from a speech made by Mountbatten when India became independent on August 15th, 1947.

Source B

> I know well that the rejoicing which your freedom brings is balanced in your hearts by the sadness that it could not come to a united India. At this historic moment, let us not forget all that India owes to Mahatma Gandhi—the architect of her freedom. In your first prime Minister, Pandit Jawaharlal Nehru, you have a world renowned leader of courage and vision. His trust and friendship have helped me beyond measure.

4. How fully does **Source B** describe the background to the granting of independence to India in 1947?

   You must use **evidence from the source** and **your own knowledge** and give reasons for your answer.

   5

[END OF CONTEXT IIIB]

Marks

UNIT III—PEOPLE AND POWER

CONTEXT C: RUSSIA 1914–1941

SECTION A: KNOWLEDGE AND UNDERSTANDING

Early in 1917, Russia collapsed into Revolution.

1. Explain why revolution broke out in Russia in March 1917.

4

Popular discontent with War Communism convinced Lenin that a change in government economic policy was necessary.

2. Describe Lenin's New Economic Policy.

3

SECTION B: ENQUIRY SKILLS

The following sources relate to Stalin's rule.

**Study the sources carefully and answer the questions which follow.
You should use your own knowledge where appropriate.**

Source A is an extract from Lenin's Testament which he dictated shortly before he died.

Source A

Comrade Stalin, having become Secretary, has unlimited authority concentrated in his hands. I am not sure whether he will be capable of using that authority with sufficient caution. Stalin is too rude and this defect, although quite tolerable in our midst and in dealings between Communists, becomes intolerable in a General Secretary. For this reason, I suggest that comrades think about a way to remove Stalin from that post and replace him with someone who has greater tolerance.

3. Discuss Lenin's view of Stalin as shown in **Source A**.

4

Marks

Source B is from "Russia and the USSR, 1905–1956" by Nigel Kelly.

Source B

> Many of those who were "purged" on Stalin's orders were loyal Communists with years of service to the party. Often they simply could not believe what was happening to them and were convinced that some terrible mistake had been made. The majority of Stalin's victims were ordinary people such as teachers and factory workers who had for some, usually unknown, reason fallen out with the authorities. Few of the victims actually wanted to overthrow Communism or replace Stalin.

4. How fully does **Source B** describe the Purges which took place under Stalin?

   You must use **evidence from the source** and **your own knowledge** and give reasons for your answer.   5

[END OF CONTEXT IIIC]

Marks

UNIT III—PEOPLE AND POWER

CONTEXT D: GERMANY 1918–1939

SECTION A: KNOWLEDGE AND UNDERSTANDING

After the end of the war, there was chaos in many German cities.

1. Describe what happened during the Spartacist revolt in Berlin.   3

The opportunities presented by the Reichstag fire were too good for the Nazis to miss.

2. Explain why the Reichstag fire helped the Nazis.   4

SECTION B: ENQUIRY SKILLS

The following sources are about young people in Nazi Germany.

**Study the sources carefully and answer the questions which follow.
You should use your own knowledge where appropriate.**

In **Source A**, a German writes about his memories of school days in Nazi Germany.

Source A

Although we were meant to, no one in our class ever read Mein Kampf. I myself only took quotations down from the book. On the whole we didn't know much about Nazi ideology. Even anti-Semitism was brought in rather marginally at school. Nevertheless, we were politically programmed to obey orders, to learn the soldierly virtue of standing to attention and to stop thinking when the magic word "Fatherland" was mentioned.

3. Discuss the attitude of the author of **Source A** towards Nazi education.   4

Marks

Source B is a photograph of members of the Hitler Youth in the 1930s.

Source B

4. How fully does **Source B** show why children were attracted to Nazi Youth organisations?

   You must use **evidence from the source** and **your own knowledge** and give reasons for your answer.

   5

[END OF CONTEXT IIID]

[END OF QUESTION PAPER]

[BLANK PAGE]

[BLANK PAGE]

G

1540/402

| NATIONAL QUALIFICATIONS 2004 | WEDNESDAY, 12 MAY 10.20 AM – 11.50 AM | HISTORY STANDARD GRADE General Level |

Answer questions from Unit I **and** Unit II **and** Unit III.

Choose only **one** Context from each Unit and answer Sections A **and** B. The Contexts chosen should be those you have studied.

The Contexts in each Unit are:

Use the information in the sources, and your own knowledge, to answer the questions.

Number the questions as shown in the question paper.

Some sources have been adapted or translated.

SCOTTISH
QUALIFICATIONS
AUTHORITY

THB 1540/402 6/29720

Marks

UNIT I—CHANGING LIFE IN SCOTLAND AND BRITAIN

CONTEXT A: 1750s–1850s

SECTION A: KNOWLEDGE AND UNDERSTANDING

Study the information in the sources. You must also use your own knowledge in your answers.

Source A is about population increase in Scotland between 1750 and 1850.

Source A

> The death rate declined across Scotland. The last serious national famine had badly affected Scotland and had killed perhaps one in seven people. From then on starvation was not a major problem. The ending of famine can be put down to improved poor relief and special emergency procedures.

1. Explain why the death rate in Scotland went down between 1750 and 1850.   **4**

Source B describes some effects of the enclosing of fields.

Source B

> In the county of Galloway, early Improving Landlords made small farms into large units and this meant several evictions. As well as this, the enclosure of parks and common land took away from the peasants their old rights of pasture. This made some people desperate.

2. What was the importance of the Enclosure Movement in Scotland?   **4**

Marks

SECTION B: ENQUIRY SKILLS

The issue for investigating is:

In the nineteenth century, cotton mills brought many benefits for people in Scotland.

Study the sources carefully and answer the questions which follow.

You should use your own knowledge where appropriate.

Source C was written in 1835 by Andrew Ure, a cotton manufacturer.

Source C

In my recent tour around many cotton factories, I have seen thousands of old, young and middle-aged of both sexes working there. Many of them were too feeble to get a job in any other kind of industry. However, they are now earning enough for good food and clothes without having to break into sweat. In a cotton mill they are also sheltered from the summer sun and the winter frost.

3. How useful is **Source C** for investigating the nineteenth century cotton mills?   3

Source D was written by Rev. Robert Boog in the Old Statistical Account for Paisley in 1791.

Source D

It is painful to think that a cotton mill which gives employment to so many people and which is a source of wealth, may lead to very unhappy effects upon the health of the children employed in it. The breathing of air loaded with the dust and downy particles of cotton must prove hurtful to their tender lungs. Some mills are kept going day and night. The children get little or no education.

4. What evidence in **Source C** agrees with the view that the cotton mills brought benefits for Scottish people?

    What evidence in **Source D** does **not** agree with the view that the cotton mills brought benefits for Scottish people?   5

5. How far do you agree that the nineteenth-century cotton mills brought benefits for Scottish people?

    You must use evidence **from the sources** and **your own knowledge** to come to a conclusion.   4

[END OF CONTEXT IA]

Now turn to the Context you have chosen in Unit II.

UNIT I—CHANGING LIFE IN SCOTLAND AND BRITAIN

CONTEXT B: 1830s–1930s

SECTION A: KNOWLEDGE AND UNDERSTANDING

Study the information in the sources. You must also use your own knowledge in your answers.

Source A gives information about Scotland's growing population.

Source A

> The population grew each year between 1830 and 1920. People at the time gave many reasons for the rise in numbers. Some said a better, more varied diet led to stronger, healthier babies. Medical knowledge also improved greatly during the period. The link between filth and disease became better understood. Clean water was increasingly supplied to towns and cities.

1. Explain why the population of Scotland increased between 1830 and 1920.   **4**

Source B describes changes in farming.

Source B

> Farming was changing. More and more open fields were being enclosed. New steam powered machinery was appearing. The use of such machinery led to fewer jobs on the land. Wages stayed low, or even fell. More and more men left for jobs in the cities. Even city slums appeared better than working 12 or 14 hours a day, in all weathers.

2. What was the importance of new machinery for working conditions on farms after 1830?   **4**

Marks

SECTION B: ENQUIRY SKILLS

The issue for investigating is:

> The coming of the railways was welcomed by people in Scotland.

Study the sources carefully and answer the questions which follow.

You should use your own knowledge where appropriate.

Source C is from the "Oban Telegraph", 10th September 1880.

Source C

> The year 1880 is truly a great one in the history of Oban. The arrival of the Callander and Oban Railway has brought great prosperity to the town. The opening of the rail route has increased trade and boosted local businesses, particularly our hotels and lodging houses. There has been no halt in the numbers of visitors and the cry is "they still come!"

3. How useful is **Source C** for investigating the impact of railways in Scotland?   3

Source D is from "British Economic and Social History" by Philip Sauvain.

Source D

> The economic effects of the railways were felt throughout the nineteenth century. The most dramatic change was the immediate decline of the stage coach with many jobs lost, especially by mail operators. As soon as a new railway link was opened, the corresponding coach service was drastically reduced. Turnpike roads fell into disuse and grass began to grow in the roadways. Owners of coaching inns went bankrupt.

4. What evidence is there in **Source C** that railways were welcomed by people in Scotland?

   What evidence is there in **Source D** that railways were not welcomed by people in Scotland?   5

5. How far do you agree that the coming of railways was welcomed by people in Scotland?

   You must use evidence **from the sources** and **your own knowledge** to come to a conclusion.   4

[END OF CONTEXT IB]

Now turn to the Context you have chosen in Unit II.

Marks

UNIT I—CHANGING LIFE IN SCOTLAND AND BRITAIN

CONTEXT C: 1880s–Present Day

SECTION A: KNOWLEDGE AND UNDERSTANDING

Study the information in the sources. You must also use your own knowledge in your answers.

Source A is about population growth.

Source A

> The population of Scotland has grown steadily over the last hundred years. After 1880 many Scottish couples married younger and had larger families. As conditions improved, more of these children survived. Also, older people lived longer and enjoyed healthier lives. However, the population did not rise as sharply as some people expected as many couples chose to limit family size.

1. Explain why Scotland's population grew over most of the period from 1880 to the present day. 4

Source B describes the decline of Scottish shipbuilding after the Second World War.

Source B

> World War Two had revived Scottish shipbuilding but, by the late 1950s, some shipyards began to close as there was less demand for ships. A world slump in 1955 affected Scotland more than her rivals. Often other countries were building vessels quicker and cheaper. Scotland could not compete with such stiff foreign competition. Instead, Scottish yards stuck to old ways of working.

2. What was the importance of foreign competition in the decline of Scottish shipbuilding after World War Two? 4

Marks

SECTION B: ENQUIRY SKILLS

The issue for investigating is:

> The First World War improved work opportunities for Scottish women.

Study the sources carefully and answer the questions which follow.

You should use your own knowledge where appropriate.

Source C was written in 1916 by Eunice Murray who had been a Suffragette in Scotland.

Source C

> After the war, men will speedily forget the fine work done by women. They will not think about the work she has done in factory and office during the war but that she is still employed at **his** job—she is a competitor with him. Men's natural instinct will be to expel women from the work place and that is what will happen.

3. How useful is **Source C** for investigating work opportunities for women during the First World War?

3

Source D is from a history textbook written by Faith Geddes in 2002.

Source D

> In 1918 women were expected to stop war time work and return home. However, there were still new job opportunities with the development of light industries and service industries such as banking. The 1919 Sex Discrimination Act ended legal restrictions on women entering universities. More women trained for professional jobs. It became more common for women to have a career and marry at a later age. Female trade union membership grew.

4. What evidence in **Source C** does **not** agree with the view that the First World War will improve work opportunities for Scottish women?

What evidence in **Source D** agrees with the view that work opportunities for Scottish women improved after the First World War?

5

5. How far do you agree that the First World War improved work opportunities for Scottish women?

You must use evidence **from the sources** and **your own knowledge** to come to a conclusion.

4

[END OF CONTEXT IC]

Now turn to the Context you have chosen in Unit II.

Marks

UNIT II—INTERNATIONAL COOPERATION AND CONFLICT

> ### CONTEXT A: 1790s–1820s

SECTION A: KNOWLEDGE AND UNDERSTANDING

Study the information in the sources. You must also use your own knowledge in your answers.

Source A is a description of the First Coalition which fought against France.

Source A

> Between 1793 and 1797 the First Coalition against France consisted of Spain, Holland, Britain, Austria and Sardinia. On land, the French armies defeated the Coalition armies. These French armies had a real will to win. The Coalition's soldiers were well trained but had no personal interest in the result. They were not interested in the territorial gains over which Prussia and Austria squabbled.

1. Describe the problems which faced the First Coalition in their war against France.   **3**

Source B describes the Congress System established after the final defeat of Napoleon.

Source B

> The Congress System was mainly the idea of Britain's representative at the Congress of Vienna, Lord Castlereagh. He thought that if all countries could meet in Congresses, the Great Powers might learn to cooperate and settle affairs at meetings. What had been, and still was, a military alliance against France might be made into a permanent and bloodless method of settling disputes.

2. Explain the reasons for setting up the Congress System.   **3**

Marks

SECTION B: ENQUIRY SKILLS

The following sources are about the war at sea.

Study the sources carefully and answer the questions which follow.

You should use your own knowledge where appropriate.

Source C was written by a French sea captain after the Battle of Trafalgar.

Source C

> All our rigging was cut to pieces. Our masts were damaged by thousands of shot from British cannons. The guns in our upper deck had all been blown off their mounts. I was wounded by a splinter. On our starboard side, nearly 450 men were killed or wounded. We were on our own against five enemy ships which were firing their cannon into us.

3. How useful is **Source C** as evidence of naval warfare in the early nineteenth century?   3

Source D is from "Battle at Sea" by John Keegan.

Source D

> As the British ship "Victory" passed slowly through the enemy lines her gunners fired at the French ship, Bucentaure. The effect of several thousand balls of shot was devastating. The torrent of shattered metal and wood from dismounted guns killed or disabled dozens of men. As each British ship passed, they repeated the deadly fire.

4. How far do **Sources C** and **D** agree on the methods of naval warfare used in the Napoleonic War?   4

5. How fully do **Sources C** and **D** show what it was like serving on a warship during the Napoleonic War?

   You must use evidence **from the sources** and **from your own knowledge** and give reasons for your answer.   4

[END OF CONTEXT IIA]

Now turn to the Context you have chosen in Unit III.

Marks

UNIT II—INTERNATIONAL COOPERATION AND CONFLICT

CONTEXT B: 1890s–1920s

SECTION A: KNOWLEDGE AND UNDERSTANDING

Study the information in the sources. You must also use your own knowledge in your answers.

Source A is from "The Origins of World War One" by Roger Parkinson.

Source A

> In order to stop Russia's advance in the Far East, an Alliance was signed between Britain and Japan in 1902. Russia, in turn, moved closer to France. Britain was alarmed at this and began to draw up its own agreement with France. It was eventually signed in 1904.

1. Describe Britain's relationships with other European powers between 1902 and 1914.   **3**

Source B is the beginning of the Covenant of the League of Nations.

Source B

> The High Contracting Parties (all the nations signing) agree to the Covenant of the League of Nations, in order to promote international cooperation and to achieve international peace and security:
>> by open and just relations between nations,
>> by the firm establishment of the understandings of international law.

2. Explain why the League of Nations was set up.   **3**

Marks

SECTION B: ENQUIRY SKILLS

The following sources are about the weapons used in trench warfare.

Study the sources carefully and answer the questions which follow.

You should use your own knowledge where appropriate.

Source C was taken by an official British Government photographer at Ovillers on the Somme in 1916.

Source C

3. How useful is **Source C** as evidence of methods of fighting in the First World War ?   **3**

Source D is from "The First World War" by S.L. Case.

Source D

> No single weapon provided a means of breaking out of the trenches. The Vickers machine gun could fire an ammunition belt of 600 rounds in 10 seconds but it was not a mobile, attacking weapon. Gas was also largely ineffective because it was an easy weapon to counter.

4. How far do **Sources C** and **D** agree about methods of fighting in the First World War?   **4**

5. How fully do **Sources C** and **D** describe the new weapons of trench warfare used in the First World War?

   You must use evidence **from the sources** and **from your own knowledge** and give reasons for your answer.   **4**

[END OF CONTEXT IIB]

Now turn to the Context you have chosen in Unit III.

Marks

UNIT II—INTERNATIONAL COOPERATION AND CONFLICT

CONTEXT C: 1930s–1960s

SECTION A: KNOWLEDGE AND UNDERSTANDING

Study the information in the sources. You must also use your own knowledge in your answers.

Source A is from "The Era of the Second World War" by Josh Brooman.

Source A

> When Germany invaded Poland this marked the start of a major war. On 3rd September, Britain and France honoured their promise to help Poland by declaring war on Germany. This also brought war with Italy, Germany's ally. As Britain and France had empires in Africa, Asia and the Far East, the war would soon spread from Europe to other parts of the world.

1. Describe what happened in Europe in the months after Germany invaded Poland.　　3

Source B is from the United Nations Charter, 1945.

Source B

> We are determined to save succeeding generations from the evil of war which twice in our lifetime has brought misery to mankind.
>
> Our aims are:
> to achieve international cooperation in solving international problems;
> to promote respect for human rights.

2. Explain why the United Nations was set up.　　3

Marks

SECTION B: ENQUIRY SKILLS

The following sources are about new technology during the Second World War.

Study the sources carefully and answer the questions which follow.

You should use your own knowledge where appropriate.

Source C is an official photograph taken during the Second World War. It shows radar operators plotting information about enemy aircraft in a bomb-proof operations room.

Source C

3. How useful is **Source C** as evidence of the use of new technology during the Second World War?

3

In **Source D** Corporal Avis Hearn describes her work during World War Two.

Source D

> I was one of the first WAAFs to train as a radar operator. At 1.00pm on 18th August 1940 our screens showed a big air raid building up over France. I was ordered to the bomb-proof building and soon a phone call told me that enemy raiders were approaching. I could not leave my post as so much information was coming in from the radar for us to plot up.

4. How far do **Sources C** and **D** agree about methods of dealing with enemy air raids in the Second World War?

4

5. How fully do **Sources C** and **D** describe the use of new British technology in the Second World War?

You must use evidence **from the sources** and **from your own knowledge** and give reasons for your answer.

4

[END OF CONTEXT IIC]

Now turn to the Context you have chosen in Unit III.

Marks

UNIT III—PEOPLE AND POWER

| CONTEXT A: USA 1850–1880 |

SECTION A: KNOWLEDGE AND UNDERSTANDING

Study the information in the sources. You must also use your own knowledge in your answers.

Source A describes the work of the "Underground Railroad" in helping slaves.

Source A

> Late one night in 1849, a 29 year old slave named Harriet Tubman escaped from her owner and the terrible treatment she had received. With the help of people in the Underground Railroad she hid by day and travelled by night until she reached freedom in Philadelphia.

1. What was the importance of the "Underground Railroad" to black slaves in the South? **3**

Source B is from "The American West" by T. Boddington.

Source B

> At first American emigrants settled in areas of the West where they could farm as they had done in the East. Then, in 1858 gold was discovered in the mountain and plateau regions of what would become Colorado and Nevada. A new gold rush began. Adventurous prospectors set off from the eastern states and travelled west. "Pike's Peak or Bust!" was the familiar phrase written on the canvas of miners' wagons.

2. Why did westward expansion increase in the years 1850–1880? **3**

Marks

SECTION B: ENQUIRY SKILLS

The following sources are about attitudes towards Reconstruction in the South.

Study the sources carefully and answer the questions which follow.

You should use your own knowledge where appropriate.

Source C is from the Report on the Joint Committee on Reconstruction, June 1866.

Source C

> A claim for the immediate admission of senators to Congress from the people of the so-called Confederate States seems to this committee not to be lawful. The Southern states had no legal right to separate themselves from the Union. It must not be forgotten that the people of these states, without any reason, rose in rebellion.

3. What is the attitude of the Joint Committee towards the people in the Southern states?   **3**

Source D is from "The Civil War, 1815–1869" by Sally Senzell Isaacs.

Source D

The Freedmen's Bureau built schools for Black Americans all over the South. Many White Southerners did not want freed slaves to get an education. This woodcut picture was made to show an attack on a school in Memphis, Tennessee in 1866.

4. How fully does **Source D** describe the problems faced by Black Americans in the South during the period of Reconstruction?

   You must use evidence **from the sources** and **from your own knowledge** and give reasons for your answer.   **4**

[END OF CONTEXT IIIA]

Marks

UNIT III—PEOPLE AND POWER

CONTEXT B: INDIA 1917–1947

SECTION A: KNOWLEDGE AND UNDERSTANDING

Study the information in the sources. You must also use your own knowledge in your answers.

Source A is from "Hind Swaraj", written by Gandhi in 1909.

Source A

> Passive resistance is superior to the force of arms. Even a man weak in body is capable of offering this resistance. One man can offer it just as well as millions. Both men and women can do it. Control over the mind is alone necessary and when it is attained, man is free like the king of the forest. His very glance withers the enemy.

1. Explain why Gandhi adopted non-violent methods of resistance. 3

Source B is from "Gandhi" by J. Simkin.

Source B

> Gandhi's response to the Direct Action massacres was to take his followers to as many villages as possible. He placed a satyagrahi in each village and instructed them to keep the peace. In some cases this worked but still the killing went on. Direct Action had the desired effect. The British government became convinced that a united India was impossible. Lord Mountbatten was appointed to sort things out.

2. What was the importance of Muslim Direct Action in bringing about independence for India? 3

Marks

SECTION B: ENQUIRY SKILLS

The following sources are about the partition of India and its effects upon Indians.

Study the sources carefully and answer the questions which follow.

You should use your own knowledge where appropriate.

In **Source C** a member of the Indian army describes his feelings towards partition.

Source C

> To us it was the heartbreak of heartbreaks. We felt it was beyond belief. We had united these dozens of different castes, creeds, colours and beliefs under one flag. We had united them under one regimental colour. It took us two hundred years to build that up and for all that to go—literally at one stroke of a pen—it was something I will never get over.

3. What was the attitude of the author of **Source C** towards the partition of India?   3

Source D is from "Growing Up in the People's Century" by John D. Clare.

Source D

The creation of an independent India and Pakistan led to millions of people becoming refugees. The photograph shows Muslims fleeing to Pakistan and Hindus fleeing to India.

4. How fully does **Source D** describe the problems faced by people after the partition of India?

   You must use evidence **from the sources** and **from your own knowledge** and give reasons for your answer.   4

[END OF CONTEXT IIIB]

Marks

UNIT III—PEOPLE AND POWER

CONTEXT C: RUSSIA 1914–1941

SECTION A: KNOWLEDGE AND UNDERSTANDING

Study the information in the sources. You must also use your own knowledge in your answers.

Source A is from a letter sent by the famous Russian writer, Leo Tolstoy, to the Tsar.

Source A

> The numbers of police, regular and secret, are continually growing. The prisons and penal colonies are overcrowded with thousands of convicts and political prisoners, among whom are some industrial workers. Censorship has reached a level not known since the 1840s.

1. Why was it so difficult to oppose the Tsar?　　3

Source B was written by an American journalist who was in Russia during the 1920s.

Source B

> As a result of the New Economic Policy the economic condition of Moscow may be considered to be better than the rest of Russia. However, similar if slower improvements are taking place in other Russian towns. Industrial workers are better off although they are hit by high prices and short-time work in many industries. At least they get paid regularly now. Industrial workers in Moscow still grumble about overcrowding.

2. How important was the New Economic Policy in improving the lives of the people of Russia?　　3

Marks

SECTION B: ENQUIRY SKILLS

The following sources are about Russia and the First World War.

Study the sources carefully and answer the questions which follow.

You should use your own knowledge where appropriate.

Source C was written by a resident of St Petersburg in 1914.

Source C

> Those first days of the war! How full we were of enthusiasm, of the certainty that we were fighting for a just cause: for the freedom of the world. Swept away by excitement, we dreamt dreams of triumph and victory. We were the Russian Steamroller. With the British navy and the French guns, the war would be over by Christmas and the Cossacks would ride into Berlin.

3. What was the attitude of the author of **Source C** to the outbreak of the First World War?

3

Source D is from "Russia and the USSR 1900–1995" by Tony Downey.

Source D

In this painting of life in Moscow in 1917, the sign in the shop window reads "No bread will be distributed today". Women had to queue for hours in the freezing cold for food.

4. How fully does **Source D** describe the problems faced by Russian civilians during the First World War?

   You must use evidence **from the sources** and **from your own knowledge** and give reasons for your answer.

4

[END OF CONTEXT IIIC]

Marks

UNIT III—PEOPLE AND POWER

| CONTEXT D: GERMANY 1918–1939 |

SECTION A: KNOWLEDGE AND UNDERSTANDING

Study the information in the sources. You must also use your own knowledge in your answers.

Source A is about the abdication of Kaiser Wilhelm II in 1918.

Source A

> There was nothing that the Kaiser could do to control the country, for the army generals refused to support him. All he could do was abdicate. On 10 November, he secretly left Germany and went by train to Holland, never to return. Only now would the Allies agree to a ceasefire.

1. Explain why the Kaiser abdicated in November 1918.

3

Source B was written by Erna von Pustau about her time in Hamburg in the 1920s.

Source B

> We were deceived too. We used to say, "All of Germany is suffering from hyperinflation". It was not true—there is no game in the world where everyone loses; someone has to be the winner. The winners during inflation were big business men in the cities and landowners in the countryside. The great losers were the working class and the middle class who had most to lose. I remember going to the baker in the morning and buying two rolls for 20 marks. In the afternoon the same rolls were 25 marks.

2. How important was hyperinflation as a cause of discontent for Germans during the 1920s?

3

Marks

SECTION B: ENQUIRY SKILLS

The following sources are about young people in Nazi Germany.

Study the sources carefully and answer the questions which follow.

You should use your own knowledge where appropriate.

Source C is part of a private letter written to a friend by a member of Hitler Youth in 1936.

Source C

> We practically don't have a minute of the day to ourselves. This isn't camp life, no sir! It's a military barrack life. Drill starts right after a simple breakfast. We would like to have athletics but there isn't any. Instead we have military exercises, down in the mud, till the tongue hangs out of your mouth. Any spare hours are filled with lectures where they tell you things you've heard hundreds of times before. We only have one wish: sleep, sleep, sleep!

3. What is the attitude of the author of **Source C** towards Hitler Youth activities?   3

Source D is from Robert Gibson and John Nicol "Germany" p.36.

Source D

Nazi Youth Movements stressed the importance of health and fitness. This photograph shows girls who were members of Jungmadel (Young Maidens) in 1936.

4. How fully does **Source D** describe what was expected of girls in Hitler's Germany?

You must use evidence **from the sources** and **from your own knowledge** and give reasons for your answer.   4

[END OF CONTEXT IIID]

[END OF QUESTION PAPER]

[BLANK PAGE]

[BLANK PAGE]

C

1540/403

NATIONAL
QUALIFICATIONS
2004

WEDNESDAY, 12 MAY
1.00 PM – 2.45 PM

HISTORY
STANDARD GRADE
Credit Level

Answer questions from Unit I **and** Unit II **and** Unit III.

Choose only **one** Context from each Unit and answer Sections A **and** B. The Contexts chosen should be those you have studied.

The Contexts in each Unit are:

Number the questions as shown in the question paper.

Some sources have been adapted or translated.

SCOTTISH
QUALIFICATIONS
AUTHORITY

©

Marks

UNIT I—CHANGING LIFE IN SCOTLAND AND BRITAIN

CONTEXT A: 1750s–1850s

SECTION A: KNOWLEDGE AND UNDERSTANDING

Farming life was transformed by new technology.

1. Why did new farming technology change the working lives of Scottish farmers in the period 1750–1850?

    4

Many factors affected the health of the British people in the first half of the nineteenth century.

2. How important was clean water in improving people's health in the first half of the nineteenth century?

    5

SECTION B: ENQUIRY SKILLS

The issue for investigating is:

There was little support for the militant Radical Movement in the period 1815–1830.

Study the sources carefully and answer the questions which follow.
You should use your own knowledge where appropriate.

Source A is from a booklet called "The Pioneers: A Tale of the Radical Rising at Strathaven in 1820". It was written by an anonymous Radical who had to flee to the West Indies to escape arrest.

Source A

Though our various Radical risings were premature, we were intent on a coordinated revolt. I remember James Wilson (a leading Radical) saying "We are twenty-five brave fellows marching for the political liberty of Scotland. We cannot afford to lose our cause." I was also inspired by another Radical saying "We can no longer submit to our shameful, political state. Let us stand and fight like men".

Marks

Source B is from "The Scottish Nation 1700–2000" by Professor T. M. Devine.

Source B

> The year 1816 was one of unrest due to high food prices. The veteran Radical, Cartwright, embarked on a Scottish tour to argue for political change. The Glasgow gathering attracted 40,000 people, the greatest political assembly that had ever taken place in Scotland. While most were reformist and moderate, placing emphasis on the petitioning of parliament, many wore the Red Cap of Liberty and demanded political change through revolution.

Source C describes events in 1819–1820.

Source C

> When economic depression returned in 1819, Radical activity increased. This alarmed the government who launched a campaign of repression against all public meetings. In England, this caused the Peterloo Massacre in Manchester which frightened many Radicals. In Scotland, secret societies continued to meet. They planned to overthrow the government by physical force. A General Strike was called and was supported by 60,000 workers from many trades. One group of Radicals decided to march to the Carron Iron Works to seize some cannons. However, this unlikely expedition ended at Bonnymuir.

3. How useful are **Sources A** and **B** for investigating the Radical Movement between 1815 and 1830? **4**

Look at Sources A, B and C.

4. What evidence is there in the sources to support the view that there was little support for the militant Radical Movement in the period 1815–1830?

   What evidence is there in the sources that there was support for the militant Radical Movement in the period 1815–1830? **6**

5. How true is it to say that between 1815 and 1830 there was little support for the militant Radical Movement?

   You must use **evidence from the sources** and **your own knowledge** to reach a **balanced conclusion**. **5**

[END OF CONTEXT IA]

Marks

UNIT I—CHANGING LIFE IN SCOTLAND AND BRITAIN

| CONTEXT B: 1830s–1930s |

SECTION A: KNOWLEDGE AND UNDERSTANDING

> Technological changes had a huge effect on the Scottish coal mining industry.

1. Why did new mining technology change the working lives of Scottish miners in the period 1830–1930?

   4

> Many factors affected the health of the British people in the period 1850–1900.

2. How important was a clean water supply in improving people's health in the second half of the nineteenth century?

   5

SECTION B: ENQUIRY SKILLS

The issue for investigating is:

> Militant tactics damaged the cause of votes for women before 1914.

Study the sources carefully and answer the questions which follow.
You should use your own knowledge where appropriate.

Source A is from "Twentieth Century Britain" written in 1977 by the historians Dennis Richards and Anthony Quick.

Source A

> In 1912 Christabel Pankhurst organised a systematic campaign of violence. Actions of this kind, however, only offended the majority of the population and made it impossible for the Prime Minister, Mr Asquith, to grant the vote to women without appearing weak. While militant actions did force men to consider the suffrage issue, by 1913 the moderate suffrage campaigners were making a much deeper impression by their propaganda than the Pankhursts were by their various outrages.

Marks

Source B is from "Memories of Helen Crawford", a Scottish member of the Women's Social and Political Union.

Source B

> In March 1912 the Suffragettes adopted more drastic methods. Although the death of Emily Davison shocked and horrified many, the heroism of many women militants called forth admiration, and an increase in the membership of the Suffrage Societies. The respectable, non-militant societies had neither the dramatic nor the spectacular appeal of the Women's Social and Political Union. Mrs Pankhurst's arrest and her hunger striking made many new recruits.

Source C is from the "Dundee Advertiser", 22nd July, 1914.

Source C

> The militant groups have carried the struggle into the midst of the people of Scotland. In doing this they have taught us much that we had been ignorant of. Twelve months ago, a militant Suffragette could not receive a hearing. She was hooted and bawled at as if she were a fanatic. Now, large crowds nightly assemble to hear and express sympathy with her. No one can stand and listen to the details of the sufferings of those in prison and remain unmoved.

3. How useful are **Sources A** and **B** for investigating the impact of militant tactics on women's struggle for the vote?   4

Look at Sources A, B and C

4. What evidence is there in the sources that militant tactics damaged women's struggle for the vote?

   What evidence is there in the sources that militant tactics helped women's struggle for the vote?   6

5. To what extent did militant tactics damage the cause of votes for women before 1914?

   You must use **evidence from the sources** and **your own knowledge** to reach a **balanced conclusion**.   5

[END OF CONTEXT IB]

Mark

UNIT I—CHANGING LIFE IN SCOTLAND AND BRITAIN

CONTEXT C: 1880s–Present Day

SECTION A: KNOWLEDGE AND UNDERSTANDING

> Twentieth-century developments in road transport brought benefits but also posed problems for society.

1. Why did developments in road transport affect the lives of people in Scotland in the twentieth century?

4

> Many factors affected the health of the British people in the twentieth century.

2. How important was slum clearance in improving people's health in the period 1890–1939?

5

SECTION B: ENQUIRY SKILLS

The issue for investigating is:

> Militant tactics damaged the cause of votes for women before 1914.

Study the sources carefully and answer the questions which follow.
You should use your own knowledge where appropriate.

Source A is from "Twentieth Century Britain" written in 1977 by the historians Dennis Richards and Anthony Quick.

Source A

> In 1912 Christabel Pankhurst organised a systematic campaign of violence. Actions of this kind, however, only offended the majority of the population and made it impossible for the Prime Minister, Mr Asquith, to grant the vote to women without appearing weak. While militant actions did force men to consider the suffrage issue, by 1913 the moderate suffrage campaigners were making a much deeper impression by their propaganda than the Pankhursts were by their various outrages.

Source B is from "Memories of Helen Crawford", a Scottish member of the Women's Social and Political Union

Source B

> In March 1912 the Suffragettes adopted more drastic methods. Although the death of Emily Davison shocked and horrified many, the heroism of many of the women militants called forth admiration, and an increase in the membership of the Suffrage Societies. The respectable, non-militant societies had neither the dramatic nor the spectacular appeal of the Women's Social and Political Union. Mrs Pankhurst's arrest and her hunger striking made many new recruits.

Source C is from the "Dundee Advertiser", 22nd July, 1914.

Source C

> The militant groups have carried the war into the midst of the people of Scotland. In doing this they have taught us much that we had been ignorant of. Twelve months ago, a militant Suffragette could not receive a hearing. She was hooted and bawled at as if she were a fanatic. Now, large crowds nightly assemble to hear and express sympathy with her. No one can stand and listen to the details of the sufferings of those in prison and remain unmoved.

3. How useful are **Sources A** and **B** for investigating the impact of militant tactics on women's struggle for the vote? **4**

Look at Sources A, B and C

4. What evidence is there in the sources that militant tactics damaged women's struggle for the vote?

   What evidence is there in the sources that militant tactics helped women's struggle for the vote? **6**

5. To what extent did militant tactics damage the cause of votes for women before 1914?

   You must use **evidence from the sources** and **your own knowledge** to reach a **balanced conclusion**. **5**

[END OF CONTEXT IC]

Marks

UNIT II—INTERNATIONAL COOPERATION AND CONFLICT

> ### CONTEXT A: 1790s–1820s

SECTION A: KNOWLEDGE AND UNDERSTANDING

> It was the foreign rather than the domestic policy of France which finally brought about war.

1. How important was French aggression as a cause of war breaking out between Britain and France in 1793? **4**

> In 1815, the twenty-two year struggle against the France of the Revolution and the Empire was at last over.

2. Describe the terms imposed on France at the Congress of Vienna in 1815. **3**

SECTION B: ENQUIRY SKILLS

The following sources are about the effect of war on the civilian population in Britain.

Study the sources carefully and answer the questions which follow.
You should use your own knowledge where appropriate.

Source A describes the effects of the Napoleonic Wars on Shetland.

Source A

> This was the period of the Press Gangs and Shetland paid a heavy price in men—possibly one third of the entire male population served at sea—mostly in the Navy. The wars closed many existing European markets for fish, which meant increasing hardship. This was also a period of hard winters and poor harvests.

3. How fully does **Source A** show the problems experienced by people in Scotland during the Napoleonic Wars?

   You must use evidence **from the source** and from **your own knowledge** and give reasons for your answer. **5**

Marks

Source B is compiled from statistics presented to parliament in the late eighteenth and early nineteenth century.

Source B

Table showing Enclosure Acts and average wheat prices in England.

Year	Number of Enclosure Acts passed	Average price of wheat (in shillings)
1792	38	41
1796	75	76
1808	91	79
1812	133	122
1819	44	72

4. How useful is **Source B** as evidence of the problems facing British people during the wars against France?

4

Source C is taken from "The Changing Face of Britain" by Paul Shuter and John Child.

Source C

> The number of Enclosure Acts increased during the war years and the common land rapidly disappeared. Grain output increased by 40% during the wartime decades but, as always, not everyone benefited equally. Landowners could charge more rent to tenant farmers as well as making bigger profits on land they farmed themselves. Farm labourers, however, were lucky if their wages increased as fast as food prices. During the years of bad harvests between 1809 and 1811 wheat and thus bread prices rose much faster than wages. Not till peace came could the public enjoy cheaper food prices.

5. To what extent do **Sources B** and **C** agree that there was hardship in Britain during the wars against France?

4

[END OF CONTEXT IIA]

Marks

UNIT II—INTERNATIONAL COOPERATION AND CONFLICT

CONTEXT B: 1890s–1920s

SECTION A: KNOWLEDGE AND UNDERSTANDING

> The British people were very worried by the growth of the German navy.

1. How important was the growth of the German navy as a cause of World War One?　　**4**

> "The Germans must pay to their last farthing and we shall search their pockets for it."
> David Lloyd George

2. Describe the economic terms imposed on Germany by the Treaty of Versailles.　　**3**

SECTION B: ENQUIRY SKILLS

The following sources are about the effects of the First World War on civilians in Britain and Germany.

**Study the sources carefully and answer the questions which follow.
You should use your own knowledge where appropriate.**

Source A is from a leaflet published by the No-Conscription Fellowship in May, 1916.

Source A

> Conscription is now law in this country. Our liberties have now been attacked. We are now under military dictation. We cannot assist in the war.
>
> #### War is wrong
>
> Conscience, it is true, has been recognised in the Conscription Act, but it has been placed at the mercy of tribunals.
>
> #### Repeal the Act
>
> If this is not done military control and government restrictions will increase in every aspect of our national life.

3. How fully does **Source A** show the opinions of British civilians in World War One towards the conduct of the government?

   You must use evidence **from the source** and from **your own knowledge** and give reasons for your answer.　　**5**

Marks

Source B is from the Illustrated London News of March, 1918.

Source B

A CONTRAST INDEED!
BRITISH AND GERMAN FOOD SUPPLIES

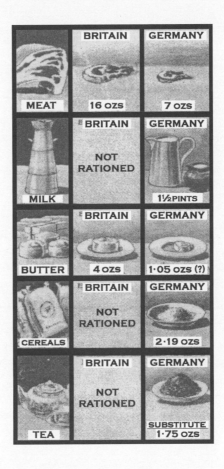

4. How useful is **Source B** as evidence of the ways in which World War One affected civilian populations?

4

Source C is from "World War One" by S. R. Gibbons and P. Morican.

Source C

> The food shortage in Britain was beginning to make itself really felt by the last year of the war. The government took action to ensure fair distribution of food throughout the community. Sugar was rationed, quickly followed by meat and fats. However, the starving Berliners would gladly have changed places with the Londoners queuing for food in 1918. Many foods had long been scarce in Germany and only ersatz coffee was available on the rations. There was a flourishing trade in potato peelings.

5. How far do **Sources B** and **C** agree about the effects of food shortage during World War One?

4

[END OF CONTEXT IIB]

Marks

UNIT II—INTERNATIONAL COOPERATION AND CONFLICT

CONTEXT C: 1930s–1960s

SECTION A: KNOWLEDGE AND UNDERSTANDING

> On Sunday, 3rd September 1939, Neville Chamberlain announced "this country is at war with Germany".

1. How important was German rearmament in the 1930s as a cause of the Second World War?

4

> The USA decided that it was not going to disappear from world affairs in 1945 as it had done in 1919.

2. Describe the changing role of the USA in world affairs after 1945.

3

SECTION B: ENQUIRY SKILLS

The following sources are about the impact of the Second World War on civilians.

Study the sources carefully and answer the questions which follow.
You should use your own knowledge where appropriate.

Source A was written by the British anti-war campaigner Fenner Brockway.

Source A

> I hated the war but I was too conscious of the evils of Nazism to be completely pacifist. However, I could not support the war effort in any way. I could see everyone around me supremely engaged in "doing their bit" but I could not join in. I felt quite alone. I complained about the whole nature of the war but the only other grumbles I heard were about the blackout or the black market.

3. How fully does **Source A** show the effects of World War Two on civilians?

You must use evidence **from the source** and from **your own knowledge** and give reasons for your answers.

5

Marks

Source B is based on official British and German Government statistics of civilian casualties due to air raids during the Second World War.

Source B

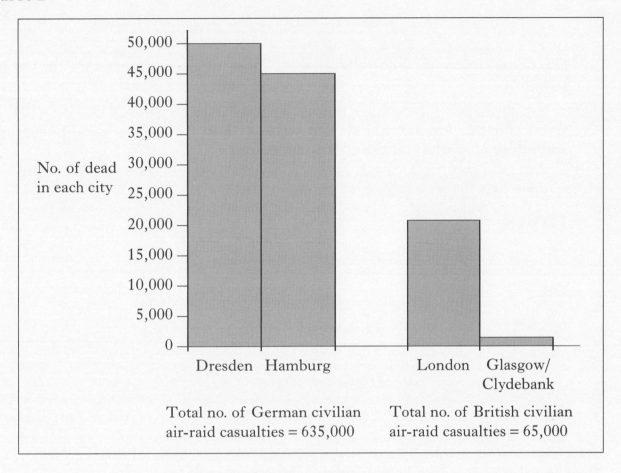

4. How useful is **Source B** as evidence of the impact of air raids on civilians during the Second World War?

4

Source C is taken from "The Home Front" by Stewart Ross.

Source C

Thousands of civilians were killed by air raids in both Britain and Germany. On the night of 14/15 November 1940 the Germans made one of the heaviest raids of the war on the city of Coventry. There were 558 casualties and the cathedral was left in ruins. Although the German policy of aerial bombardment destroyed 86,000 homes and killed over 60,000 civilians it did not seriously affect British morale. British and American raids were far heavier and took more lives, especially in Hamburg in 1943 and Dresden in 1945.

5. To what extent do **Sources B** and **C** agree about the effects of air raids on civilians during the Second World War?

4

[END OF CONTEXT IIC]

Marks

UNIT III—PEOPLE AND POWER

CONTEXT A: USA 1850–1880

SECTION A: KNOWLEDGE AND UNDERSTANDING

> To loyal citizens on both sides the Civil War was a just war: one that had to be fought.

(Note: for this answer you should write a short essay of several paragraphs including an introduction and a conclusion.)

1. Explain fully the reasons for going to war in 1861

   EITHER

   (*a*) from the viewpoint of the Northern states   **8**

   OR

   (*b*) from the viewpoint of the Southern states.   **8**

SECTION B: ENQUIRY SKILLS

The following sources are about the effects of westward expansion on native Americans.

**Study the sources carefully and answer the questions which follow.
You should use your own knowledge where appropriate.**

Source A is part of a speech made to the United States Commissioners by Ten Bears, a Comanche chief, in 1867.

Source A

> There are things you have said to me which were not sweet like sugar but bitter like gourds. You said you wanted to put us upon a reservation and to build us houses. I do not want them. I was born upon the prairie where the wind blew free and there was nothing to break the light of the sun. When I was at Washington, the Great Father told me that all Comanche land was ours. Do not ask us now to give up the buffalo for the sheep.

2. Discuss the attitude of Ten Bears towards the US Commissioners.   **4**

Marks

Source B is from a Treaty between Comanche Indians and the Commissioners of the United States of America.

Source B

> The United States agrees to construct buildings including a warehouse and a residence for a physician.
>
> The head of each family shall be entitled to receive seeds and animals and receive instructions from a farmer.
>
> The tribe will agree to withdraw all opposition to the construction of the railroad now being built across the plains.
>
> No member of the tribe will attack any persons nor disturb any wagon train, coaches, mules or cattle.

3. How far do **Sources A** and **B** agree about the treatment of Comanche Indians on the Great Plains? **4**

[END OF CONTEXT IIIA]

Marks

UNIT III—PEOPLE AND POWER

CONTEXT B: INDIA 1917–1947

SECTION A: KNOWLEDGE AND UNDERSTANDING

The main problem was not granting self rule but the conflict between the Congress Party and the Muslim League.

(Note: for this answer you should write a short essay of several paragraphs including an introduction and a conclusion.)

1. Explain fully the reasons for Indians supporting

   EITHER

   (a) the Congress Party   8

   OR

   (b) the Muslim League.   8

SECTION B: ENQUIRY SKILLS

The following sources relate to the effects of British rule on India.

**Study the sources carefully and answer the questions which follow.
You should use your own knowledge where appropriate.**

Source A is part of a letter which Gandhi wrote to the Viceroy in March, 1930.

Source A

British rule has made millions of Indians poor by using their country's wealth for the benefit of the British. They also set up a very large Civil Service and an army which the country can never afford. British rule has reduced us to slavery. It has destroyed our culture. My ambition is to convert the British people through non-violence and to make them see the wrongs they have done to my country. It seems as clear as daylight that British statesmen will not make any change to British policy that might harm Britain's trade with India.

2. Discuss the attitude of Gandhi in **Source A** towards British rule in India.   4

Marks

Source B is from "Plain Tales from the Raj" by Charles Allen.

Source B

> The British found India in a state of chaos and anarchy and with very low moral standards. They established in time a common language, a legal system and a civil service of rare quality. They also provided the great civilising effect of the Indian Army. The British did indeed bring uninterrupted peace—though not prosperity—within India's borders.

3. How far do **Sources A** and **B** agree about the effects of British rule on India?　　4

[END OF CONTEXT IIIB]

Marks

UNIT III—PEOPLE AND POWER

> ### CONTEXT C: RUSSIA 1914–1941

SECTION A: KNOWLEDGE AND UNDERSTANDING

> The official historians of the USSR have tended to describe the Bolshevik victory as if it were inevitable.

(Note: for this answer you should write a short essay of several paragraphs including an introduction and a conclusion.)

1. Explain fully the reasons for the Bolshevik success in

   EITHER

   (*a*) seizing power in October 1917   **8**

   OR

   (*b*) winning the Civil War 1917–1921.   **8**

SECTION B: ENQUIRY SKILLS

The following sources are about the collectivisation of Russian farming.

**Study the sources carefully and answer the questions which follow.
You should use your own knowledge where appropriate.**

Source A was written by Lev Kopelev.

Source A

> With the rest of my generation, I firmly believed that the end justified the means. I saw what collectivisation meant—how they mercilessly seized everything from the peasants. I took part in it myself, searching the countryside and testing the earth for loose spots that might lead to buried, hidden grain. With others, I emptied old folks' storage chests of food. For I was convinced that I was accomplishing the great and necessary transformation of the countryside; that in days to come people who lived there would be better off.

2. Discuss the attitude of the author of **Source A** towards collectivisation.   **4**

Marks

Source B is from "Russia and the USSR, 1900–1995" by Tony Downey.

Source B

> When appeals for change did not work, Stalin adopted a policy of forced collectivisation. He began by trying to force food from the peasants. Young, enthusiastic party workers went round the countryside looking for food. They believed that the peasants were hiding supplies. Any food they found was confiscated by the party. There were riots against this forced requisitioning of food and the next year there was even less food available.

3. To what extent do **Sources A** and **B** agree about the policy of collectivisation?

4

[END OF CONTEXT IIIC]

Marks

UNIT III—PEOPLE AND POWER

> ### CONTEXT D: GERMANY 1918–1939

SECTION A: KNOWLEDGE AND UNDERSTANDING

> While in prison, Hitler came to the conclusion that the Nazis would have to work within the democratic system to achieve power.

(Note: for this answer you should write a short essay of several paragraphs including an introduction and a conclusion.)

1. Explain fully the reasons why the Nazis were able to come to power in 1933 as a result of

EITHER

(*a*) their own actions and activities   8

OR

(*b*) the failures of the Weimar Government.   8

SECTION B: ENQUIRY SKILLS

The following sources are about opposition to the Nazis.

**Study the sources carefully and answer the questions which follow.
You should use your own knowledge where appropriate.**

Source A was written by Werner Best, Gestapo Deputy Chief in the late 1930s.

Source A

> Nazi belief in totalitarianism does not tolerate the development of any political opposition. Any attempt to gain support for opposing ideas will be ruthlessly dealt with, as the symptoms of an illness which threatens the healthy unity of the State. To discover the enemies of the state, to watch them and make them harmless is the duty of the political police. In order to achieve this task, the political police must be free to use every means necessary.

2. Discuss the attitude of the author of **Source A** towards opposition to the Nazis.   4

Marks

Source B is from "Modern World History" by Ben Walsh.

Source B

> Any opposition to Nazi rule was unacceptable to the Nazi authorities and all political opponents of the Nazis were thrown into concentration camps. This began as early as 1934. This made it very difficult for these groups to organise resistance to the Nazis and they were easy prey for the political police. Despite the Concordat with the Catholic Church, many individual priests did resist the Nazis and this led them to being dealt with harshly. One priest who gave an anti-Nazi sermon was visited by the SS who smashed up his church and beat him up.

3. To what extent do **Sources A** and **B** agree about opposition to Nazi rule? **4**

[END OF CONTEXT IIID]

[END OF QUESTION PAPER]

[BLANK PAGE]

2005 | General

[BLANK PAGE]

G

1540/402

NATIONAL QUALIFICATIONS 2005	MONDAY, 16 MAY 10.20 AM – 11.50 AM	HISTORY STANDARD GRADE General Level

Answer questions from Unit I **and** Unit II **and** Unit III.

Choose only **one** Context from each Unit and answer Sections A **and** B. The Contexts chosen should be those you have studied.

The Contexts in each Unit are:

You must use the information in the sources, and your own knowledge, to answer the questions.

Number the questions as shown in the question paper.

Some sources have been adapted or translated.

SCOTTISH
QUALIFICATIONS
AUTHORITY

©

Marks

UNIT I—CHANGING LIFE IN SCOTLAND AND BRITAIN

CONTEXT A: 1750s–1850s

SECTION A: KNOWLEDGE AND UNDERSTANDING

Study the information in the sources. You must also use your own knowledge in your answers.

Source A is from the Old Statistical Account for Gargunnock in Stirlingshire, written in 1797.

Source A

> Great improvement is being made in the art of ploughing. Prizes are given annually by the wealthy land owners in the area to those who plough best and the tenant farmers eagerly compete for this honour. The Old Scots Plough is most generally used but Small's new plough is beginning to be preferred. A threshing machine has been set up by some farmers. It is one of the most useful farming machines ever invented.

1. How important was new technology in Scottish farms in the late eighteenth century?   **4**

Source B describes housing in the Scottish countryside.

Source B

> The form of dwelling most often seen was the longhouse or byre-dwelling. This, in its later eighteenth-century form, consisted of a drystone-built structure with an interior divided into living quarters and space for cattle. The floor was usually of stamped earth with the fireplace in the centre of the floor.

2. Describe housing in the Scottish countryside in the eighteenth century.   **3**

Marks

SECTION B: ENQUIRY SKILLS

The issue for investigating is:

> Moving from the countryside to the town was good for all Scots in the period 1750–1850.

Study the sources carefully and answer the questions which follow.

You should use your own knowledge where appropriate.

Source C was written in the early nineteenth century by Gilbert Burns, brother of Robert Burns, the famous poet.

Source C

> I often heard our father describe the sadness he felt when he had to leave *his* father's farm and move away. He and his brother parted on top of a hill overlooking their beloved countryside, each going off in search of employment. Our father first moved to Edinburgh where he found employment. There was no work on the farm and those were difficult times for farmers. Farming was an uncertain business then and many were forced to move away from the countryside.

3. How useful is **Source C** for investigating population movement in Scotland between 1750 and 1850?　　3

Source D is from "The Scottish Nation" by T. M. Devine.

Source D

> In 1750 only one tenth of the Scottish population lived in towns. By 1850 more Scots lived in towns than in almost any other country in Europe. Newspapers were remarking on the number of workers leaving the countryside or coming down from the Highlands, driven as much by misery at home as by new opportunities and employment in the Lowland towns. Scottish factory owners needed to attract such migrants and population movement was a bonus for manufacturers keen to hire more labour.

4. What evidence is there in **Source C** that moving from the countryside to the town was **not** good for Scottish people?

   What evidence is there in **Source D** that moving from the countryside to the town was good for Scottish people?　　5

5. How far do you agree that moving from the countryside to the town was good for all Scots in the period 1750–1850?　　4

   You must use evidence **from the sources** and **your own knowledge** to come to a conclusion.

[END OF CONTEXT IA]

Now turn to the Context you have studied in Unit II

UNIT I—CHANGING LIFE IN SCOTLAND AND BRITAIN

CONTEXT B: 1830s–1930s

SECTION A: KNOWLEDGE AND UNDERSTANDING

Study the information in the sources. You must also use your own knowledge in your answers.

Source A is about the effects of new technology on the early days of railways.

Source A

> The idea of railway tracks was not new. Wagonways with wooden rails had been used to make it easier to move horse-drawn trucks carrying coal. Several inventions helped to create the Railway Age and, by 1832, steam locomotives were in regular use enabling trains to travel at over 30 miles an hour. Greater speeds were also made possible by the development of heavier steel rails and improvements in signalling made travelling safer.

1. How important was new technology in the development of railways?   **4**

Source B describes housing in an area of the Scottish countryside in the nineneenth century.

Source B

> It was quite unusual for farm workers to settle in a farm for much more than two or three years. They lived in tied cottages provided as part of the deal on pay. Most farm workers' dwellings were single roomed. The walls were less than two metres high. There was no ceiling as such. The room was divided inside by wooden box beds.

2. Describe housing in the Scottish countryside in the nineteenth century.   **3**

Marks

SECTION B: ENQUIRY SKILLS

The issue for investigating is:

> The arrival of Irish immigrants brought benefits for all Scots.

Study the sources carefully and answer the questions which follow.

You should use your own knowledge where appropriate.

Source C is evidence given to a Parliamentary Enquiry in 1836 by Alexander Carlisle who ran a spinning mill in Paisley.

Source C

> Our mills never would have grown so rapidly if we had not had large numbers of Irish families. The work of this town requires women and children as well as men. Without the Irish, a sufficient number of workers would never have been found. The large immigration of the Irish at the harvest season also proves a great advantage to our farmers.

3. How useful is **Source C** for investigating the results of Irish immigration into Scotland?

3

Source D is from "Changing Life in Scotland and Britain".

Source D

> Many native Scots resented the Irish. They accused them of dragging down wages. While this was undoubtedly true, it has to be counterbalanced by saying that by 1880 they were becoming prominent in Trade Unions and were helping to push up wages. However, the arrival of large numbers of desperately poor Irish did nothing to ease the already overcrowded housing situation. Moreover, their arrival sometimes increased existing tensions over religious beliefs and practices.

4. What evidence is there in **Source C** that the arrival of Irish immigrants brought benefits?

   What evidence is there in **Source D** that the arrival of Irish immigrants did **not** bring benefits?

5

5. How far do you agree that the arrival of Irish immigrants brought benefits for all Scots?

4

   You must use evidence **from the sources** and **your own knowledge** to come to a conclusion.

[END OF CONTEXT IB]

Now turn to the Context you have studied in Unit II

Marks

UNIT I—CHANGING LIFE IN SCOTLAND AND BRITAIN

CONTEXT C: 1880s–Present Day

SECTION A: KNOWLEDGE AND UNDERSTANDING

Study the information in the sources. You must also use your own knowledge in your answers.

Source A is from "Change in Scotland, 1830–1930" by W. Doran and R. Dargie, published in 1994.

Source A

> The Equal Pay Act said men and women should be paid the same wage for doing the same work. Between 1970 and 1975 women's earnings rose from 63% to 72% of men's wages. They have remained about the same ever since. Some employers got round this by transferring women to jobs where there are no male workers to compare themselves with.

1. How important was the introduction of new laws in improving employment and working conditions for women? **4**

In **Source B** Jean Whittle describes living in a house in the countryside near Jedburgh in the 1920s.

Source B

> We lived in one part of a house, with my father's parents. There was always an apprentice lived with us. Quite often there would be fifteen of us in the building. I well remember how the grown-ups were served their meals first. The water had to be carried into the house from a tap a few yards away. There was a separate building called the "wash house" where the scrubbing of clothes was done.

2. Describe housing in the countryside in early twentieth-century Scotland. **3**

Marks

SECTION B: ENQUIRY SKILLS

The issue for investigating is:

> The arrival of immigrants was good for Scotland.

Study the sources carefully and answer the questions which follow.

You should use your own knowledge where appropriate.

In **Source C** Mary McEwan writes about the 1930s in "I Can Remember", published in 1976.

Source C

> The Italians in Glasgow were always friendly. I liked their cafes which stayed open a' the time and sold fags, ice cream and fish and chips. I loved to sit in them wi' ma friends and listen to the waiters chattering in Italian and many girls went out with them later. It brought a new dimension to the drab city. It was somewhere warm and cheerful away frae ma single end (house).

3. How useful is **Source C** for investigating the impact of immigrants on Scotland?　　3

Source D is from "The Scottish Nation" by T.M. Devine.

Source D

> A Parliamentary Committee suggested that Italian ice-cream parlours were lowering moral standards as the owners allowed young people of both sexes to meet there after proper opening hours and sometimes misbehave themselves. After closing time, at 10.00 pm on a Saturday in Glasgow, many went to buy their fish suppers. The food was not always consumed peacefully and the police had to be called to control fights. However, all in all, the Italians attracted much less hostility than did the Irish and the Lithuanians.

4. What evidence in **Source C** agrees with the view that the arrival of immigrants was good for Scotland?

   What evidence in **Source D** disagrees with the view that the arrival of immigrants was good for Scotland?　　5

5. How far do you agree that the arrival of immigrants was good for Scotland?　　4

   You must use evidence **from the sources** and **your own knowledge** to come to a conclusion.

[END OF CONTEXT IC]

Now turn to the Context you have studied in Unit II

Marks

UNIT II—INTERNATIONAL COOPERATION AND CONFLICT

CONTEXT A: 1790s–1820s

SECTION A: KNOWLEDGE AND UNDERSTANDING

Study the information in the sources. You must also use your own knowledge in your answers.

Source A is from "The Fourth Coalition" by Peter Lane.

Source A

> There was a brief break in the years of warfare during most of 1813. Napoleon used this opportunity to build up a new army, but it now contained many poorly trained men. Meanwhile, the Austrians, Prussians and Russians joined Britain in the Fourth Coalition. The Allied armies closed in on Napoleon's troops who were then defeated at the Battle of the Nations in October.

1. Explain why the Fourth Coalition was able to defeat Napoleon. 3

Source B is from the National Maritime Museum's website.

Source B

> Punishments at sea were designed as warnings to others. Of course, some captains were more cruel than others but even Admiral Nelson, who cared for his men, found it necessary to condemn sailors to harsh floggings. Seamen could also be "tarred and feathered" or tied to a rope, swung overboard and dragged round the underneath of the ship.

2. How important was harsh punishment as a cause of complaint on board ships in Nelson's navy? 4

Marks

SECTION B: ENQUIRY SKILLS

The following sources are about the Congress of Vienna.

Study the sources carefully and answer the questions which follow.

You should use your own knowledge where appropriate.

Source C was written by Lewis Goldsmith in 1822.

Source C

> The monarchs and important ministers at the Congress of Vienna were almost wholly occupied by promoting their own power and strength. They neglected to take measures for preserving future peace. They showed the most unfortunate ignorance of public feeling. They should have known that people do not like being moved from ruler to ruler.

3. What did Lewis Goldsmith think about the Congress of Vienna?   **3**

Source D is about the Congress of Vienna and is from "www.napoleonguide.com".

Source D

> The powerful delegates at Vienna decided not to punish France too severely. While a workable peace was the main aim, the delegates also wanted to restore the legitimate rulers of Europe and to increase their power. Prussia and Russia wanted to divide up Saxony and this annoyed Austria. Poland was now ruled by the Russian tsar and many Poles were unhappy.

4. To what extent do **Sources C** and **D** agree about the Congress of Vienna?   **4**

[END OF CONTEXT IIA]

Now turn to the Context you have studied in Unit III

Marks

UNIT II—INTERNATIONAL COOPERATION AND CONFLICT

CONTEXT B: 1890s–1920s

SECTION A: KNOWLEDGE AND UNDERSTANDING

Study the information in the sources. You must also use your own knowledge in your answers.

Source A is from "The First World War" by John Keegan.

Source A

> Almost one month after they had been blamed for the assassinations at Sarajevo, the Serbian government received the ultimatum from Austria-Hungary. At first, they thought they would have to give in and accept all ten points. However, on hearing that Russia was very much on their side, they decided to attach conditions to six points and to reject absolutely the most important point. On hearing this, Austria-Hungary declared war on Serbia.

1. Explain why Austria-Hungary went to war against Serbia in 1914. 3

Source B is from "Landships" by David Fletcher.

Source B

> The British tanks, in three great waves, rolled down on the German defences at Cambrai. Working to a pre-arranged pattern, the tanks easily crossed the main trench lines and pushed on, with the German infantry scattering before them. However, if the success came as a surprise to the Germans, the British Command were also surprised as they had not expected such a breakthrough and had no reserves to exploit it.

2. How important was the tank as a weapon in the First World War? 4

Marks

SECTION B: ENQUIRY SKILLS

The following sources are about the Treaty of Versailles.

Study the sources carefully and answer the questions which follow.

You should use your own knowledge where appropriate.

Source C was written by British Prime Minister, David Lloyd George, about the Treaty of Versailles.

Source C

> I cannot imagine any greater cause of war than surrounding the German people with a number of small states containing large masses of Germans demanding reunion with their native land. The Treaty will strip Germany of her colonies and reduce her army to a mere police force. If Germany feels she has been unjustly treated she will seek revenge.

3. What did Lloyd George think about the Treaty of Versailles?   3

Source D is from "Mein Kampf" by Adolf Hitler.

Source D

> In the year 1919, the German people were burdened with the unjust peace treaty. You would have thought that the cry for German freedom would have been loudly promoted by the government but it was not. The Treaty was a shame and a disgrace. It must be our aim to get back to Germany the land and the people to which we are entitled. State boundaries are made by man and can be changed by man and *we will* change them when our army is restored to its full strength.

4. How far do **Sources C** and **D** agree about the Treaty of Versailles?   4

[END OF CONTEXT IIB]

Now turn to the Context you have studied in Unit III

UNIT II—INTERNATIONAL COOPERATION AND CONFLICT

CONTEXT C: 1930s–1960s

SECTION A: KNOWLEDGE AND UNDERSTANDING

Study the information in the sources. You must also use your own knowledge in your answers.

Source A describes the effects of German rearmament.

Source A

> In 1934 Hitler gave top secret orders for the armed forces to expand. This was forbidden by the Treaty of Versailles. In 1935 Hitler cast off the cloak of secrecy and announced that there would be compulsory military service. The countries around Germany were alarmed and quickly began making alliances with each other in case Germany attacked one of them.

1. Explain why German rearmament led to increased tension in Europe.   **3**

Source B describes when the Atom bomb was dropped on Hiroshima on 6th August 1945.

Source B

> The bomb fell for 53 seconds and exploded at about 1800 feet above the ground. What followed was the greatest man-made explosion ever seen at that time. More than 60,000 buildings were destroyed as a huge fire storm raged across the city. Possibly 80,000 were killed and thousands were injured as a giant mushroom cloud rose over the city.

2. How important was the use of the Atom bomb in the conduct of the war against Japan?   **4**

Marks

SECTION B: ENQUIRY SKILLS

The following sources are about the Cuban Missile Crisis.

Study the sources carefully and answer the questions which follow.

You should use your own knowledge where appropriate.

Source C was written by the Russian leader, Khrushchev, in his memoirs.

Source C

> One thought kept hammering away at my brain: "What will happen if we lose Cuba?" If Cuba fell, other Latin American countries would reject us. I had to answer the American threat but still avoid war. I had the idea of putting missiles on Cuba without letting the United States know. Our missiles would, I thought, stop America from taking action against Cuba's government. As well as protecting Cuba, the Americans would also learn what it feels like to have enemy missiles pointing at you.

3. What was Khrushchev's opinion on the placing of missiles on Cuba?   3

Source D is an American view of the Cuban Missile Crisis.

Source D

> The defence of Cuba did not really need the introduction of long-range nuclear missiles. One can be sure that Khrushchev took the decision to place missiles on Cuba, not for Cuban reasons but for Russian reasons. He would have placed 64 Soviet missiles—all effective against America. Every country in the world watching such a cheeky action, just ninety miles from the United States, would wonder whether it would ever again trust America's resolve.

4. To what extent do **Sources C** and **D** agree about why missiles were placed on Cuba?   4

[END OF CONTEXT IIC]

Now turn to the Context you have studied in Unit III

Marks

UNIT III—PEOPLE AND POWER

CONTEXT A: USA 1850–1880

SECTION A: KNOWLEDGE AND UNDERSTANDING

Study the information in the sources. You must also use your own knowledge in your answers.

Source A is about Abraham Lincoln and the Union.

Source A

> When Abraham Lincoln became President in March 1861, Fort Sumter was still under Government control. Southerners had been talking about secession for many years. Lincoln's duty as President of the United States was to protect the Constitution. Lincoln said that he must hold **all** the property belonging to the Government. He also said that he must collect **all** the taxes due to the Government.

1. Explain why Abraham Lincoln wanted to preserve the Union.   3

Source B describes the work of the Freedmen's Bureau.

Source B

> The Freedmen's Bureau had been established in 1865, while the war was still going on. It was used to supply food to ex-slaves. It also provided hospitals. The Freedmen's Bureau also supervised ex-slaves' contracts with plantation owners. It offered to rent them land that had been taken from the Confederates.

2. Describe the work of the Freedmen's Bureau after the Civil War.   3

Marks

SECTION B: ENQUIRY SKILLS

The following sources are about slavery in the South before the Civil War.

Study the sources carefully and answer the questions which follow.

You should use your own knowledge where appropriate.

Source C is a drawing which appeared in a Southern magazine before the Civil War.

Source C

Happy slaves dance on their Southern Plantation.

3. How useful is **Source C** as evidence of the conditions of slaves before 1860?   **4**

Source D is taken from a book about Civil Rights.

Source D

> Slaves were regarded as property. The point of their existence was to work for their owners. Most were given little or no education. Families could be broken up, children could be sold without their parents. Housing was often of the poorest and most basic. Many slaves were cruelly treated and lived in great unhappiness.

4. How far do **Sources C** and **D** disagree about the treatment of slaves in the South?   **3**

Source E is about slave resistance.

Source E

> Slaves did not always accept the way they were treated without protest. Slaves often tried to run away. About 1,000 slaves a year escaped. From time to time slave rebellions occurred. The possibility of such revolts terrified the South. Usually, however, protest took simpler forms. Some slaves pretended to be ill to stop them from working. Other common ways of protest were deliberately misunderstanding instructions or working slowly.

5. How fully does **Source E** describe the actions taken by slaves against their slavery?   **4**

    You must use evidence **from the sources** and **from your own knowledge** and give reasons for your answer.

[END OF CONTEXT IIIA]

Marks

UNIT III— PEOPLE AND POWER

CONTEXT B: INDIA 1917–1947

SECTION A: KNOWLEDGE AND UNDERSTANDING

Study the information in the sources. You must also use your own knowledge in your answers.

Source A is from the memoirs of a British missionary in India.

Source A

> I went to India at the age of thirty-three. Before then I never heard one single word of blame with regard to British rule in India. The idea was always impressed on me that British management of the Indian continent was the most glorious event in the whole of British History. British rule in India was indeed something I agreed with.

1. Explain why many British people agreed with British rule in India. 3

Source B is from a British military newspaper in 1919.

Source B

> India has just come out of the Great War. In the events recently seen at Amritsar, General Dyer had only his Indian troops and police to keep order. Dyer's men had toured the city for two hours. There was then an attempt by some Indians to hold a banned public meeting. As the crowd refused to disperse, the order to fire was given. There were heavy casualties amongst the mob.

2. Describe the events at Amritsar in April 1919. 3

Marks

SECTION B: ENQUIRY SKILLS

The following sources are about India before Independence.

Read the sources carefully and answer the questions which follow.

You should use your own knowledge where appropriate.

Source C is a David Low cartoon from the London Evening Standard in 1928.

Source C

UNITED INDIA.

The peoples of India are united in their opposition to British rule.

3. How useful is **Source C** as evidence of the desire for Indian Independence? 4

Source D is from "Divide and Quit" by Penderel Moon.

Source D

> The Congress Party was important to many Indians who longed for an end to British rule. Such an organisation, headed and symbolised by Gandhi, had emotional and religious appeal to the Hindu peoples but it did not always appeal to the Muslims. Gandhi often claimed that he brought all groups together: that he was "a Muslim, a Hindu, a Buddhist and a Parsee". This claim, however, was not believed by all the different religious groups in India.

4. How far do **Sources C** and **D** agree about how united the people of India were in their desire for an independent India? 3

Source E is by a modern Indian historian.

Source E

> India was within reach of its Independence. The events of the Direct Action Day shocked and split many Indian people. The Congress Party had now formed a temporary Government. Mohammed Jinnah, the leader of the Muslim League, had decided to stay away. However he nominated five of his followers to join it, with orders to wreck it from within.

5. How fully does **Source E** explain the political differences inside India before Independence? 4

You must use evidence **from the sources** and **from your own knowledge** and give reasons for your answer.

[END OF CONTEXT IIIB]

Marks

UNIT III—PEOPLE AND POWER

CONTEXT C: RUSSIA 1914–1941

SECTION A: KNOWLEDGE AND UNDERSTANDING

Study the information in the sources. You must also use your own knowledge in your answers.

Source A is from a secret Petrograd Police Report, dated October 1916.

Source A

> Military defeats have brought the people to a clearer understanding of war. It means unfair distribution of foodstuffs as well as an immense increase in the cost of living. Everywhere there are exceptional feelings of hostility and opposition to the government because of the unbearable burden of war and the worsening conditions of everyday life.

1. Explain why World War One caused growing discontent in Russia. 3

Source B is about the October Revolution in Russia.

Source B

> By 24th October the Red Guards were well armed and ready for action. During the night they began to take control of the most important locations in Petrograd. First, they took control of the six bridges across the River Neva. Then, in the morning, they seized the power station and the railway station. The Provisional Government had its headquarters in the Winter Palace and was guarded only by army cadets and the Women's Battalion.

2. Describe the main events of the Bolshevik seizure of power in October 1917. 3

Marks

SECTION B: ENQUIRY SKILLS

The following sources are about the Russian Civil War.

Study the sources carefully and answer the questions which follow.

You should use your own knowledge where appropriate.

Source C is a Bolshevik Civil War poster from 1919.

Source C

Denikin   Kolchak   Yudenich

Britain, France and the USA control the White commanders.

3. How useful is **Source C** as evidence of Russian attitudes towards the Whites during the Civil War?   **4**

Source D describes the Allied intervention in the Civil War.

Source D

> Britain, France and the USA, along with several other powers, sent help to the Whites. Allied intervention was half-hearted and ineffective and did little to help the White leaders, Kolchak, Denikin and Yudenich. The intervention of foreign countries in fact helped the Communists. They portrayed the Whites as being controlled by foreign powers, while they themselves were defenders of ordinary Russians from foreign invaders.

4. How far do **Sources C** and **D** agree about the Civil War?   **3**

In **Source E** a Red Army soldier describes the effects of Trotsky's leadership.

Source E

> The city of Gomel was about to fall into enemy hands when Trotsky arrived. Then everything changed and the tide turned. Trotsky's arrival meant that the city would not be abandoned. Trotsky paid a visit to the troops in the front lines where he made a speech. We were lifted by the energy he displayed and indeed by his very appearance wherever a critical situation arose.

5. How fully does **Source E** describe Trotsky's role in the Red Army's victory?   **4**

    You must use evidence **from the sources** and **from your own knowledge** and give reasons for your answer.

[END OF CONTEXT IIIC]

Marks

UNIT III—PEOPLE AND POWER

CONTEXT D: GERMANY 1918–1939

SECTION A: KNOWLEDGE AND UNDERSTANDING

Study the information in the sources. You must also use your own knowledge in your answers.

In **Source A** a German soldier describes his return to Frankfurt in 1918.

Source A

> In October I had permission to go home. I was very much looking forward to this leave after the terrific battles we had been through. As I went through the streets of Frankfurt I was not saluted, even though I was an officer. There was hardly anything to buy and what there was, was rationed. I hadn't realised at the front just how fed up with the war people were.

1. Explain why, by late 1918, German civilians wanted the war to end.   **3**

Source B is about the Munich Putsch.

Source B

> During a time of political and economic chaos in Germany, Hitler decided to lead an uprising. On November 8th, 1923, Herr von Kahr, head of the Bavarian government, spoke at a big meeting in a beer cellar in Munich. With some Nazi supporters, Hitler went into the meeting. He waited until 600 SA men had surrounded the building and then 25 Nazis burst into the hall. Hitler declared that a national revolution had begun.

2. Describe the main events of the Munich Putsch in November 1923.   **3**

Marks

SECTION B: ENQUIRY SKILLS

The following sources are about the methods used by the Nazis to come to power.

Study the sources carefully and answer the questions which follow.

You should use your own knowledge where appropriate.

Source C is a Nazi poster from the early 1930s.

Source C

The SA march toward Aryan purity

3. How useful is **Source C** as evidence of what people in Germany thought of the SA in the 1930s?   4

Source D is from "Hitler and Germany" by B. J. Elliot.

Source D

> Some saw in the SA an appeal to their Aryan manhood. Some were attracted by the uniforms and badges, particularly the ex-soldiers. Some were impressed by the strength portrayed by the Brownshirts. Others who were repelled by Nazism, were, quite naturally, frightened into silence. Hitler believed that the SA was his trump card and went out of his way to glorify as heroes those members who were killed or wounded.

4. To what extent do **Sources C** and **D** agree on the ways the SA was made to appeal to Germans?   3

Source E was written by an American who had attended a Nazi rally.

Source E

> The hall was a sea of brightly coloured flags. Hitler's arrival was dramatic. The band stopped playing. There was a hush over the 30,000 people packed into the hall. Hitler appeared and strode slowly down the centre aisle while 30,000 hands were raised in salute. In such an atmosphere no wonder that every word spoken by Hitler was greeted with enormous cheering.

5. How fully does **Source E** describe the appeal of Hitler to the German people in the 1930s?   4

You must use evidence **from the sources** and **from your own knowledge** and give reasons for your answer.

[END OF CONTEXT IIID]

[END OF QUESTION PAPER]

[BLANK PAGE]

[BLANK PAGE]

[BLANK PAGE]

C

1540/403

NATIONAL
QUALIFICATIONS
2005

MONDAY, 16 MAY
1.00 PM – 2.45 PM

HISTORY
STANDARD GRADE
Credit Level

Answer questions from Unit I **and** Unit II **and** Unit III.

Choose only **one** Context from each Unit and answer Sections A **and** B. The Contexts chosen should be those you have studied.

The Contexts in each Unit are:

Number the questions as shown in the question paper.

Some sources have been adapted or translated.

SCOTTISH
QUALIFICATIONS
AUTHORITY

©

Marks

UNIT I—CHANGING LIFE IN SCOTLAND AND BRITAIN

| CONTEXT A: 1750s–1850s |

SECTION A: KNOWLEDGE AND UNDERSTANDING

> In the first half of the nineteenth century, towns and cities were steadily becoming more lethal.

1. How far do you agree that cholera was the most important public health problem in Britain between 1800 and the 1850s?

5

> The Scottish electoral system in 1830 was totally unfair.

2. Describe some ways in which the 1832 Reform Act made Scotland more democratic.

3

SECTION B: ENQUIRY SKILLS

The issue for investigating is:

> Changes in textile manufacture brought major benefits for people in Scotland in the period 1750–1850.

**Study the sources carefully and answer the questions which follow.
You should use your own knowledge where appropriate.**

Source A was written by cotton manufacturer James Ogden in his "Description of Textile Manufacture" published in 1783.

Source A

> There is a huge demand for exports of textiles for foreign trade. There is also a growing demand for domestic use. No amount of effort by any number of workmen could have answered those demands without the introduction of the spinning machines. People saw how children, from nine to twelve years of age, could manage the machines easily and also bring plenty of money into families that before were poverty stricken and overburdened with children. Consequently, even more new machinery has been brought into the mills.

3. How useful is **Source A** for investigating textile manufacture in Scotland in the period 1750–1850?

4

Marks

Source B was written in "Scotland, A New History" by Professor of History, Michael Lynch, in 1992.

Source B

> The coming of cotton brought new-style discipline in the alien world of the factory for the spinners of yarn. It was an easily learned skill but practised in a hostile environment where heat and dust often caused tuberculosis. It was a trade for the young: almost two out of every three of both the male and female workforce were under twenty-one. The factory employed cheap labour from wherever it could get it. Cotton thread production brought with it an increased demand for handloom weavers.

Source C is from "Modern Scottish History" by A. Cooke and I. Donnachie, published in 1988.

Source C

> Although its aim was still to produce a more efficient and obedient workforce, Robert Owen's regime at New Lanark was better than elsewhere. There can be little doubt that, however unappealing factory work was at New Lanark, it was altogether more disagreeable elsewhere, especially in the smaller country mills and the urban factories of Glasgow and Paisley. The cotton-spinning industry grew so rapidly that by 1795 there were no fewer than ninety-one mills in Scotland.

Look at Sources A, B and C.

4. What evidence is there in the sources to support the view that changes in textile manufacture brought benefits for people in Scotland?

   What evidence in the sources **disagrees** with the view that changes in textile manufacture brought benefits for people in Scotland?　　6

5. How far do you agree that changes in textile manufacture brought major benefits for people in Scotland in the period 1750–1850?

   You must use **evidence from the sources** and **your own knowledge** to reach a **balanced conclusion**.　　5

[END OF CONTEXT IA]

Marks

UNIT I—CHANGING LIFE IN SCOTLAND AND BRITAIN

CONTEXT B: 1830s–1930s

SECTION A: KNOWLEDGE AND UNDERSTANDING

> Worsening living conditions in the towns had a profound effect upon the public.

1. How far do you agree that cholera was the biggest health problem in nineteenth-century Britain?

   5

   > Parliamentary reform in the early twentieth century marked another important step on the road to democracy.

2. Describe the ways in which the 1918 Reform Act made Britain more democratic.

   3

SECTION B: ENQUIRY SKILLS

The issue for investigating is:

> The coalmining industry brought benefits for people in Scotland in the nineteenth century.

Study the sources carefully and answer the questions which follow.
You should use your own knowledge where appropriate.

Source A is a description of the life of mine workers in Alloa, written by Robert Bald, a mining engineer in the first half of the nineteenth century.

Source A

> The collier leaves his house for the pit along with his sons about eleven o' clock at night. About three hours after, his wife sets out for the pit having wrapped her infant in a blanket and left it to the care of an old woman who keeps three or four children at a time and feeds them with ale or whisky mixed with water. The mother descends the pit with her older daughters. It is no uncommon thing to see them, when coming back up again, weeping most bitterly from the excessive severity of the labour. But the instant they have laid down their burden, they resume their cheerfulness and return down the pit singing.

3. How useful is **Source A** for investigating coalmining in Scotland in the nineteenth century?

   4

Marks

Source B is from "Changing Life in Scotland and Britain" by historians Ronald Cameron, Christine Henderson and Charles Robertson. It was published in the year 2000.

Source B

> During the nineteenth century there was a phenomenal growth in the coalmining industry due to increased demand for coal. Technological advances made it possible for more coal to be produced. New and deeper pits were developed. The production of coal became Scotland's largest industry, employing most workers. Whole new towns grew up around coalmining areas. Unfortunately, these were often places of dreadful overcrowding.

Source C is from "Years of Change" by J. Patrick and M. Packham, published in 1989.

Source C

> Miners could earn high wages. Mineowners expected them to work six days a week, but many worked only five. Even at that, their pay was nearly double that of many farm workers. But most miners lived in squalor. The women were expected to look after the home, but miners' wives also worked down the pit and had no energy to do housework. One doctor in Scotland noticed a fearful amount of filth accumulated on the walls and floors of miners' cottages.

Look at Sources A, B and C.

4. What evidence is there in the sources to support the view that coalmining brought benefits for people in Scotland?

   What evidence is there in the sources to suggest that coalmining did **not** bring benefits for people in Scotland? **6**

5. How far do you agree that the coalmining industry brought benefits for people in Scotland in the nineteenth century?

   You must use **evidence from the sources** and **your own knowledge** to reach a **balanced conclusion**. **5**

[END OF CONTEXT IB]

Marks

UNIT I—CHANGING LIFE IN SCOTLAND AND BRITAIN

CONTEXT C: 1880s–Present Day

SECTION A: KNOWLEDGE AND UNDERSTANDING

> By the early twentieth century, governments started to accept they had a role to play in improving the health of the population.

1. How far do you agree that government action was the most important factor in improving health in twentieth-century Britain?

   5

> Parliamentary reform in the early twentieth century marked another important step on the road to democracy.

2. Describe the ways in which the 1918 Reform Act made Britain more democratic.

   3

SECTION B: ENQUIRY SKILLS

The issue for investigating is:

> Changes in road transport brought benefits for people in Britain.

**Study the sources carefully and answer the questions which follow.
You should use your own knowledge where appropriate.**

Source A is from the diary of Arthur Illingworth, written in the 1930s.

Source A

> By 1934 holidays were longer and I got paid during them. The motor car had brought adventure within everyone's reach, making accessible both highways and byways. On bank holidays the roadsides were littered with fathers of families mending tyres and crawling under vehicles, but this was part of the excitement of the new motoring craze. Families motored to lakes and to the seaside. Cobbled market squares filled up with traffic.

3. How useful is **Source A** for investigating the effects of road transport on the people of Britain?

   4

Marks

Source B is an extract from "A Social and Economic History of Industrial Britain" by historian John Robottom, published in 1986.

Source B

> With every year, the number of motor vehicles increased rapidly. In addition, many towns were cut in two by roads which no one could cross safely. There was also the problem of rising health dangers from noise and fumes. One solution was to build motorways which helped traffic move faster and drew vehicles away from town bottlenecks. However, the new roads affected and often disturbed many lives. Houses were cleared to make way for them and people living near them had to use double glazing to cut down on the noise.

Source C is an extract from "A Century in Photographs – Travel" by Ian Harrison, published in 2000.

Source C

> Although Britain's motorways are now hopelessly overcrowded, they have certainly cut journey times. They have also reduced fatal accidents to less than half the level on ordinary roads, although two lorry drivers were killed in the M1's first fatal accident within a week of it opening. Motorways are notorious, too, for the damage they do to our landscape. They need an enormous amount of space and resources. Even in 1972 the cost of building a motorway was about £2 million per mile.

Look at Sources A, B and C.

4. What evidence is there in the sources that changes in road transport brought benefits for the people of Britain?

   What evidence is there in the sources that changes in road transport did **not** benefit the people of Britain?   **6**

5. How far do you agree that changes in road transport brought benefits for people in Britain in the twentieth century?

   You must use **evidence from the sources** and **your own knowledge** to reach a **balanced conclusion**.   **5**

[END OF CONTEXT IC]

Marks

UNIT II—INTERNATIONAL COOPERATION AND CONFLICT

CONTEXT A: 1790s–1820s

SECTION A: KNOWLEDGE AND UNDERSTANDING

> "The British Isles are declared to be in a state of blockade." Article 1 of the Berlin Decrees, 1806.

1. Explain why the French Wars affected the lives of British civilians. 4

> Castlereagh intended the Congresses to have very limited functions.

2. Describe the difficulties faced by the Congress System in keeping international peace between 1815 and 1825. 4

SECTION B: ENQUIRY SKILLS

The following sources are about the causes of the Revolutionary War.

Study the sources carefully and answer the questions which follow.
You should use your own knowledge where appropriate.

Source A is from a speech given by Prime Minister William Pitt to the House of Commons in February, 1793.

Source A

> The highly provocative French decrees of late 1792 promised military assistance to any European people wishing to depose its rulers. Now, the French nation is insisting upon the opening of the River Scheldt. We cannot stand by as indifferent spectators while France tramples upon the ancient treaties of our allies. We cannot view with indifference the progress of French ambition and of French arms. We must declare our resolution to oppose the ambitions of a nation which has murdered its monarch and which will destroy Britain, Europe and the World.

3. How useful is **Source A** as evidence of why Britain went to war with France in 1793? 4

Source B is from "Modern British History" by G.W. Southgate.

Source B

> The killing of Louis XVI destroyed any sympathy which many had felt for a people struggling for liberty. The Edict of Fraternity might have resulted in war but a French agent in London offered an explanation of the Edict which postponed the crisis. However, the opening of the River Scheldt to navigation, in defiance of international treaties, made a conflict unavoidable.

4. How far do **Sources A** and **B** agree about the causes of the French Revolutionary War? 5

[END OF CONTEXT IIA]

Marks

UNIT II—INTERNATIONAL COOPERATION AND CONFLICT

CONTEXT B: 1890s–1920s

SECTION A: KNOWLEDGE AND UNDERSTANDING

> Soldiers on the Western Front went through an enormous range of experiences.

1. Explain why the experiences of soldiers on the Western Front changed their attitudes towards the war.

    4

> "The work of the League of Nations will be fair and just, but it will need the support of the combined power of the great nations." President Woodrow Wilson, 1919.

2. Describe the difficulties faced by the League of Nations in keeping international peace between 1919 and 1928.

    4

SECTION B: ENQUIRY SKILLS

The following sources are about the causes of the First World War.

**Study the sources carefully and answer the questions which follow.
You should use your own knowledge where appropriate.**

Source A was written by Herbert Sulzbach in his diary on August 1st, 1914.

Source A

> Our Glorious Kaiser has ordered general mobilisation of the army and navy. Try as I might, I can't convey the splendid spirit and wild enthusiasm that has come over us all. We have always felt that Russia was going to attack us and now the idea that we are going to be able to defend ourselves gives us unbelievable strength. Russia's dirty intrigues are dragging us into this war; the Kaiser warned the Russians as late as 30th July. I still can't imagine what it's going to be like—putting the Russians, and hopefully the British Navy, in their places.

3. How useful is **Source A** as evidence of international tensions before the outbreak of World War One?

    4

Source B is part of a speech made by David Lloyd George in 1914.

Source B

> Have you heard the Kaiser's speeches? They are full of the bluster of German militarism, full of phrases like "mailed fist" and "shining armour". There is the same swagger and boastfulness running through every speech. He says "let us trample the Russians who challenge the supremacy of Germany in Europe and let us defeat Britain and take control of the seas! What will then be left?—nothing will be left except Germany:– 'Deutschland uber Alles'."

4. How far do **Sources A** and **B** disagree about the causes of World War One?

    5

[END OF CONTEXT IIB]

UNIT II—INTERNATIONAL COOPERATION AND CONFLICT

CONTEXT C: 1930s–1960s

SECTION A: KNOWLEDGE AND UNDERSTANDING

> At first the war had little effect upon people living in Germany.

1. Explain why the Second World War increasingly affected the lives of German civilians. **4**

> The Charter of the United Nations Organisation was signed on August 4th, 1945.

2. Describe the difficulties faced by the United Nations in keeping international peace between 1945 and 1960.

4

SECTION B: ENQUIRY SKILLS

The following sources are about the Munich Conference during the Czech crisis of 1938.

**Study the sources carefully and answer the questions which follow.
You should use your own knowledge where appropriate.**

Source A is from a speech by Neville Chamberlain in the House of Commons in September 1938.

Source A

> The real triumph is that it has shown that four great powers can find it possible to agree on a way of carrying out a difficult operation by discussion instead of force of arms. The relief at our escape from war has, I think, everywhere been mingled in this country with a profound feeling of sympathy for Czechoslovakia. I have nothing to feel ashamed of. The path which leads to appeasement is long and full of obstacles. The question of Czechoslovakia is the latest and perhaps the most dangerous. Now that we have passed it, I feel it may be possible to make further progress along the road to sanity.

3. How useful is **Source A** as evidence about the agreement reached at Munich in 1938? **4**

Source B is from a speech made by Winston Churchill in the House of Commons in October 1938.

Source B

> I will begin by saying that (Neville Chamberlain) has sustained a total and unmitigated defeat. All the hopes of a long peace which lay before Europe at the beginning of 1933, when Hitler came to power, and all the opportunities of stopping the growth of Nazi power, have been thrown away. So far as this country is concerned, the responsibility must rest with those who have control of our political affairs. And do not suppose that this is the end; this is only the beginning of the reckoning.

4. How far do **Sources A** and **B** disagree about the achievements of Neville Chamberlain?

5

[END OF CONTEXT IIC]

[Turn over for Unit III on *Page twelve*]

Marks

UNIT III—PEOPLE AND POWER

CONTEXT A: USA 1850–1880

SECTION A: KNOWLEDGE AND UNDERSTANDING

> After the Civil War, the emancipated slaves of the South expected to become fully-fledged United States citizens.

(Note: for this answer you should write a short essay of several paragraphs including an introduction and a conclusion.)

1. How far would you agree that the most important problem facing Blacks in the South after the Civil War was:

   EITHER

   (*a*) the activities of the Ku Klux Klan?   **8**

   OR

   (*b*) the restrictions of the Black Codes?   **8**

SECTION B: ENQUIRY SKILLS

The following sources are about Westward expansion and its effect on the Native Americans.

Study the sources carefully and answer the questions which follow.
You should use your own knowledge where appropriate.

Source A is from a speech made by the Native American chief, Geronimo, to officials of the Government of the USA.

Source A

> We are held on lands which are not suited to our needs. Our people are decreasing in numbers here, and will continue to decrease unless they are allowed to return to their native land. There is no climate or soil which is equal to our previous home: the land which the Almighty created for us. I want to die in peace feeling that our numbers will not diminish as at present and that our name will not become extinct.

2. Discuss the attitude of the author of **Source A** towards the Government's treatment of the Native Americans.   **3**

Marks

Source B is taken from "The American West" by Mike Mellor.

Source B

> After the Battle of Little Bighorn there was no prospect of a Native American military victory against the Whites. The only option for the Plains Indians was life on a reservation. They were given small amounts of land that white people did not want. They found this hard to accept as they were hunters, not farmers. Most of the Government agents were unsympathetic to the Native Americans. Food rations were often inadequate, as were medical supplies and disease killed many. Efforts were made to destroy their culture.

3. How far do Sources A and B agree about the Government's treatment of the Native Americans?

4

Source C is from a painting produced in 1849.

Source C

4. How fully does Source C show conditions for miners during the 1849 Gold Rush?

You should use **evidence from the source** and **your own knowledge** and give reasons for your answer.

5

[*END OF CONTEXT IIIA*]

Marks

UNIT III—PEOPLE AND POWER

CONTEXT B: INDIA 1917–1947

SECTION A: KNOWLEDGE AND UNDERSTANDING

> Prime Minister Attlee appointed Lord Mountbatten to deal with all the problems involved in getting Britain out of India.

(Note: for this answer you should write a short essay of several paragraphs, including an introduction and a conclusion.)

1. How far do you agree that the most important problem facing Mountbatten was:

EITHER

   (*a*) achieving Indian independence?   **8**

OR

   (*b*) dealing with the difficulties of partition?   **8**

SECTION B: ENQUIRY SKILLS

The following sources are about Mahatma Gandhi and Indian opposition to British rule.

**Study the sources carefully and answer the questions, which follow.
You should also use your own knowledge where appropriate.**

Source A was written by Arvind Nehra, an Indian who had been educated in England.

Source A

> Gandhi's ideals are about as unattainable as those with which I left Cambridge University. I also had wanted to bring about a better understanding between Indian and British people. It had all seemed so easy at Cambridge. But it is not so. Gandhi insists that every Indian must do without foreign goods. They must wear only the native Khaddar cloth. I sat down and worked this out one night, only to discover, alas, that there would be something like three inches of Indian cotton cloth per head of population.

2. Discuss the attitude of the author in **Source A** towards Gandhi's beliefs.   **3**

Marks

Source B is from "History of the Freedom Movement in India" by R. Majumdar.

Source B

> Gandhi's personality and saintly character inspired confidence. His will and enthusiasm alone stirred the masses into action. Gandhi always had a profound attraction to the Indian mind. His ideals and wishes appealed to everyone in a manner perhaps unique in the world's history. He could exploit a spirit of blind devotion and complete obedience in every Indian—to an extent usually reserved for a spiritual guru. Whatever sacrifice he asked of the Indians was accepted.

3. How far do **Sources A** and **B** agree about Gandhi and his beliefs? **4**

Source C is a photograph from an Indian newspaper published in 1928.

Source C

4. How fully does **Source C** show Indian opposition to British rule in India in the 1920s?

    You should use **evidence from the source** and **your own knowledge** and give reasons for your answer. **5**

[END OF CONTEXT IIIB]

Marks

UNIT III—PEOPLE AND POWER

CONTEXT C: Russia 1914–1941

SECTION A: KNOWLEDGE AND UNDERSTANDING

> Stalin wanted to stay in power and change Russia.

(Note: for this answer you must write a short essay of several paragraphs, including an introduction and a conclusion.)

1. How far would you agree that the most important method Stalin used to control Russia was:

EITHER

(a) the Five Year Plans?   **8**

OR

(b) the Purges?   **8**

SECTION B: ENQUIRY SKILLS

The following sources are about the effects of the rule of Tsar Nicholas II in Russia.

Study the sources carefully and answer the questions which follow.
You should also use your own knowledge where appropriate.

Source A is from the British Ambassador in Russia to the British Government in the early months of 1914.

Source A

> Russia under Tsar Nicholas has had many problems. However, Russia is rapidly becoming powerful and is now stronger than at any time since the start of the century. The recent policies of the government have seen its metal-producing industry overtake that of Austria. Russia is now also producing thousands of tons of coal. Rapid industrialisation has led to the building of some enormous factories in St. Petersburg and Moscow. We must retain at all costs the friendship of the Tsar's great Empire.

2. Discuss the attitude of the author of **Source A** towards the Russia ruled by Tsar Nicholas.   **3**

Marks

Source B is from "Modern World History" by Ben Walsh.

Source B

> Tsar Nicholas was keen to see Russia becoming an industrial power. Policies were introduced which led to rapid industrial growth. Coal production trebled and, even more spectacularly, iron production quadrupled. Some peasants left the land to work in these new industries in cities: the heaviest concentrations being in Moscow and St. Petersburg. However, their living conditions hardly improved and other nations looked with horror at the poverty which existed in the Tsar's Russia.

3. How far do **Sources A** and **B** agree about the impact of the Tsar's rule on Russia?   4

Source C is a poster of discontented Russians during the time of Tsar Nicholas II. The Russian word used in the poster says "Bread".

Source C

„Хлеба"

4. How fully does **Source C** show discontent among Russian people in 1914?

   You should use **evidence from the source** and **your own knowledge** and give reasons for your answer.   5

[END OF CONTEXT IIIC]

Marks

UNIT III—PEOPLE AND POWER

> ### CONTEXT D: Germany 1918–1939

SECTION A: KNOWLEDGE AND UNDERSTANDING

> The Nazis faced relatively little open opposition during their twelve years in power.

(Note: for this answer you should write a short essay of several paragraphs, including an introduction and a conclusion.)

1. How far would you agree that the main reason that opposition groups in Nazi Germany failed was:

   EITHER

   (*a*) the weaknesses of the opposition groups?   **8**

   OR

   (*b*) the powers of the Nazi state?   **8**

SECTION B: ENQUIRY SKILLS

The following sources are about the treatment of the Jews and young people in Nazi Germany.

**Study the sources carefully and answer the questions which follow.
You should also use your own knowledge where appropriate.**

Source A is from the diary of a German writer, Von Hassell, who was writing on November 25th, 1938.

Source A

> I am writing under the crushing emotion evoked by the evil persecution of the Jews after the murder of Von Rath. Not since the Great War have we lost so much credit in the world. Goebbels has seldom been so disbelieved as when he said that an unplanned outburst of anger among the people had caused the outrages. As a matter of fact, there is no doubt that we are dealing with an officially organised anti-Jewish riot which broke out at the same hour of night all over Germany.

2. Discuss the attitude of the author of **Source A** towards Nazi treatment of the Jews.   **3**

Marks

Source B is from a report by the American consul in Leipzig in November 1938.

Source B

> The attacks on Jewish property, which began in the early hours, were hailed subsequently in the Nazi press as a "spontaneous wave of righteous indignation throughout Germany, as a result of the cowardly Jewish murder of Von Rath". As far as many Germans are concerned, a state of popular indignation that would lead to such excesses can be considered as non-existent. On the contrary, all of the local crowd I observed were obviously stunned over what had happened and horrified over the unprecedented fury of the Nazi acts.

3. To what extent do **Sources A** and **B** agree about attacks on the Jews?   4

Source C is a photograph showing young girls at a Nazi rally in Coburg in the 1930s.

Source C

4. How fully does **Source C** show the extent of Nazi control of young people in the 1930s?

    You should use **evidence from the source** and **your own knowledge** and give reasons for your answer.   5

[END OF UNIT IIID]

[END OF QUESTION PAPER]

[BLANK PAGE]

[BLANK PAGE]

[BLANK PAGE]

[BLANK PAGE]

[BLANK PAGE]

[BLANK PAGE]

[BLANK PAGE]

Acknowledgements

Leckie & Leckie is grateful to the copyright holders, as credited, for permission to use their material:

Wendy Doran & Richard Dargie for extracts reproduced from *Change in Scotland 1830–1930* (2003 General paper p 7, 2003 Credit paper pp 2, 4, 6, 2004 General paper pp 4, 6 and 2005 General paper p 6);

Pulse Publications for extracts from *Changing Life in Scotland and Britain* by Cameron, Henderson and Robertson (2003 Credit paper p 2, 2005 General paper pp 4, 5 and 2005 Credit paper pp 5, 10);

Getty Images for 5 photographs (2003 General p 17, 2004 General p 1, 2004 General pp 13, 19 and 2005 Credit p 13);

The David King Collection for a photograph (2003 General paper p 19);

Mary Evans Picture Library for a photograph (2003 General paper p 21) and a poster (2005 General paper p 21);

Suddeutsche de GmbH for a photograph (2003 Credit paper p 21);

Helena Shovelton for an extract from *An Illustrated History of Modern Britain, 1783-1964* by D. Richards and J.W. Hunt (2004 General paper p 8);

The Navajivan Trust for an extract from *Hind Swaraj* by Gandhi (2004 General paper p 16);

North Wind Pictures for a photograph (2004 General paper p 15);

The Illustrated London News Picture Library for a picture (2004 Credit paper p 11);

The National Maritime Museum for an extract from their website: www.nmm.ac.uk (2005 General paper p 8);

John Ray for an extract from *History for You – The Twentieth Century World* by J. Ray & J. Hagerty (2005 General paper p 12);

Adapted extracts from *Causes & Consequences of the African American Civil Rights Movement* by Michael Weber. Published by Evans Brother Ltd, 2A Portsman Mansions, Chiltern Street, London W1M 1LE. Copyright Evans Brothers Ltd © 1997. All rights reserved. (2005 General paper pp 14 & 15);

Solo Syndication for an illustration from *The London Evening Standard* (2005 General paper p 17).

The following companies/individuals have very generously given permission to reproduce their copyright material free of charge:

Pearson Education for:

an extract from *A Social and Economic History of Industrial Britain* by Robottom (2003 Credit paper p 7 and 2005 Credit paper p 7);

an extract from *International Co-Operation: The League of Nations & UNO* by Gibbons (2003 Credit paper p 11);

an extract from *The Era of the Second World War* by Josh Brooman (2004 General paper p 12);

an extract from *World War One* by Gibbons & Morican (2004 Credit paper p 11);

an extract from *Hitler's Germany 1933-1945* by Josh Brooman (2005 General paper p 12);

an extract from *The Penguin History of the United States* by Hugh Brogan (2005 General paper p 14);

an extract from *Russia in War & Revolution* by Josh Brooman (2005 General paper p 18);

an extract from *Hitler & Germany* by B.J. Elliot (2005 General paper p 21);

an extract from *Weimar Germany, 1918–1933* by Josh Brooman (2005 General paper p 21);

Extracts from *The Scottish Nation 1700–2000* by T.M. Devine (1999). Reproduced by permission of Penguin Books Ltd. (2003 Credit paper p 5, 2004 Credit paper p 3 and 2005 General pp 3 & 7);

The Inverness Courier for an extract (2003 General paper p 5);

Extract from *Mastering Modern British History* by Norman Lowe, 1998, Palgrave Publishers, reproduced with permission of Palgrave Macmillan (2003 General paper p 9);

The Hodder Wayland Picture Library for a picture (2003 General paper p 15);

Extract from *The New Penguin History of Scotland* edited by R.A. Houston and W. Knox (Allen Lane The Penguin Press, 2001) (2003 Credit paper p 3);

Extract from *A Century of the Scottish People 1560–1830*, T.C. Smout © 1972, HarperCollins Publishers Ltd. (2003 Credit paper p 5);

Columbia University Press for an extract from *The Biography of George Canning* (2003 Credit paper p 9);

John Murray (Publishers) Ltd for an extract from *Modern World History* by Ben Walsh (2003 Credit paper p 10 and 2004 Credit paper p 21);

Extract from *Making History: World History from 1914 to the Present Day* by C. Culpin © 1991, HarperCollins Publishers Ltd. (2003 Credit paper p 11);

Extract from *Black Peoples of the Americas* by Rees and Sherwood. Reprinted by permission of Harcourt Education Ltd. (2003 Credit paper p 15);

Extract from *Nehru* by Stanley Wolpert, 1996 Oxford University Press (2003 Credit paper p 17);

Extract from *Russia and the USSR 1905–1956* by Nigel Kelly. Reprinted by permission of Harcourt Education Ltd (2003 Credit paper p 19);

Hodder & Stoughton for an extract from *Years of Weimar & The Third Reich* by D. Evans & J. Jenkins (2003 Credit paper p 20);

Hodder and Stoughton for an extract from *Scotland and Britain, 1830-1980* by Chalmers and Cheyne (2004 General paper p 4);

Imprint Publishing for an extract from *Standard Grade History Revision Guide* by Faith Geddes (2004 General paper p 6);

The Scottish Library for extracts from *Bonnie Fechters: Women in Scotland 1900–1950* by S. Livingstone (2004 General paper p 7);

Dr Marjorie Bloy for an extract from *A Web of English History* (2004 General paper p 8);

Random House for two extracts from *Battle at Sea* by John Keegan (2004 General paper p 9);

Causeway Press for an extract from *The Era of the Second World War* by Tony and Steve Lancaster (2004 General paper p 13);

Extracts from *The American West, 1840-95* © T. Boddington 1977, HarperCollins Publishers Ltd. (2004 General paper p 14 and 2005 Credit paper p 12);

The BBC for an extract and photograph from *Growing up in the People's Century* by John D. Clare (2004 General paper p 17);

Time Warner for an extract from *Plain Tales from the Raj* by Charles Allan (2004 General paper p 17 and 2004 Credit paper p 17);

Extracts from *Russia and the USSR 1990-1995* by Tony Downey (1996). Reproduced by permission of Oxford University Press (2004 General paper p 19 and 2004 Credit paper p 19);

Blackwell Publishing Ltd for an extract from *Germany* by R. Gibson and J. Nichols (2004 General paper p 20);

Jonathon Nichols for a photograph from *Germany* by R. Gibson and J. Nichols (2004 General paper p 21);

An extract from *Germany 1918-1949* © A. White and E. Hadley 1990, HarperCollins Publishers Ltd. (2004 General paper p 21);

The Dundee Courier for an extract from *The Dundee Advertiser* 1914 (2004 Credit paper p 5);

The Shetland Museum for an extract from their website (2004 Credit paper p 8);

An extract from *The Changing Face of Britain* by P. Shuter & J. Child. Reprinted by permission of Harcourt Education Ltd. (2004 Credit paper p 9);

An extract from 'Indian Treaties, 1778-1883' from *The American West*, 1840-1895 © L. Knappler 1977, HarperCollins Publishers Ltd. (2004 Credit paper p 15);

Hodder & Stoughton for extracts from *Modern World History* by Ben Walsh (2004 Credit paper p 21 and 2005 Credit p 17);

Extract from *The Oxford Companion to Scottish History* by Lynch, Michael (2001). By permission of Oxford University Press (2005 General paper p 2);

Hodder & Stoughton for an extract from *Success in British History* by Peter Lane (2005 General paper p 8);

Random House for an extract from *The First World War* by John Keegan (2005 General paper p 10);

HMSO for an extract from *Landships, British Tanks in the First World War* by David Fletcher (2005 General paper p 10);

Learning & Teaching Scotland for an extract from *The House Divided – America 1850–1865* (2005 General paper p 15);

Extract from *Divide & Quit* by Sir Penderal Moon. Reproduced by permission of the Executors of the estate of Sir Penderal Moon (2005 General paper p 17);

Cambridge University Press for an extract from *Russia & the USSR* by Philip Ingram, published in 1997 (2005 General paper p 18);

Hodder & Stoughton for an extract from *Russia & The USSR 1900–1995* by Terry Fiehn (2005 General paper p 19);

Extract from *Forgotton Voices of the Great War* by Max Arthur, published by Ebury Press. Reprinted by permission of The Random House Group Ltd. (2005 General paper p 20);

Hodder & Stoughton for an extract from *People & Power: Germany* by I. Matheson (2005 General paper p 20);

Extract from *Scotland: A New History* by Michael Lynch. Reprinted by permission of The Random House Group Ltd. (2005 Credit paper p 3);

John Donald Publishers (Birlinn) Ltd for an extract from *Modern Scottish History* by A. Cooke and I. Donnachie (2005 Credit paper p 3);

Hodder & Stoughton for an extract from *Years of Change* by J. Patrick & M. Packham (2005 Credit paper p 5);

Extract from *A Century in Photographs – Travel* by Ian Harrison. Reprinted by permission of HarperCollins Publishers Ltd © Ian Harrison 2000 (2005 Credit paper p 7);

Peter Vansittart for an extract from *Voices 1870–1914* (2005 Credit paper p 9);

Express Newspapers for an extract from a speech by David Lloyd George (2005 Credit paper p 9);

Cambridge University Press for an extract from *The American West* by Mike Mellor (2005 Credit paper p 13);

Extract from *The Rise and Fall of the Great Powers* by Paul Kennedy. Reprinted by permission of HarperCollins Publishers Ltd © Paul Kennedy 1988. (2005 Credit paper p 16);

The University of Exeter Press for an extract from *Nazism 1919–1945 Volume Two: State, Economy & Society 1933-1939* edited by J Noakes & G Pridham, new edition 2000. (2005 Credit paper p 19);

Photograph courtesy of the Imperial War Museum, London (2005 Credit paper p 19).